What people are saying about …

"*Grow Together* offers a blueprint for igniting powerful spiritual growth in the church through multigenerational relationships."
–Ravi Zacharias, Author of *Why Jesus?*

"When Jesus charged us with the Great Commission, He did not say 'make *believers*' — He said 'make disciples.' How do you do that? After you read and watch *Grow Together*, you'll know how."
–Frank Turek, Author of *I Don't Have Enough Faith to Be an Atheist*

"The work of Jeff Myers and Summit Ministries is truly inspirational — they stand as bold proof that, with the right approach, the next generation is poised to be inspired and mobilized by the Gospel. More than any other efforts I know, his work encourages me about the future of young Christians."
–Nabeel Qureshi, Author of *Seeking Allah, Finding Jesus*

"This is the church's greatest moment. Here's how to make the most of it! Jeff Myers' double helix of worldview and life-on-life mentoring will be used by God to impact the church and change the world! You can have all the right truth, but if it's not lived out in relationships it will never change your family, it will never change the church, and it will never change the world. *Grow Together* explores the proven spiritual power of multigenerational mentoring."
–Josh McDowell, Author of *The Unshakeable Truth*

"I am deeply intrigued by The Grow Together Project. Jeff Myers' double helix of truth and relationship is powerful. I believe uniting the generations in the church will lead to a thrilling new season of influence for God's people."
–J.P. Moreland, Author of *Love Your God With All Your Mind*

GROW
TOGETHER

JEFF MYERS

**The Forgotten Story of How
Uniting the Generations
Unleashes Epic
Spiritual
Potential**

Summit Ministries, Manitou Springs, CO 80829
www.summit.org
© 2014 by Jeffrey L. Myers
All rights reserved. Published 2014

Printed in the United States of America
First printing 2014

ISBN-10: 0-936163-31-3
ISBN-13: 978-0-936163-31-4
Library of Congress PCN: 2014950997

I'd like to thank

my loving and supportive family, our Summit and church communities, my dear friends — old and new, and the dozens of caring adults who personally invested in my life and helped give shape to my soul. May your cultivation yield abundant fruit generation after generation.

This entire project emerged out of a seedling nonprofit organization called Passing the Baton International. Thank you particularly to John, Paul, Christie, J.R. and Mark for helping give shape to the vision, and to Roger, Paul, Paige, Sean, John and Tony for helping bring it to life.

I'm humbled by the feedback, insight, encouragement and financial support that brought the Grow Together project to reality. To the Van Eerden, Krupa, Thompson, Drake and Zimmerman families, this is for you. May thousands upon thousands in the emerging generation come alive as a result of your touch.

CONTENTS

1

HOW THE GENERATIONAL DIVIDE GRINDS DOWN THE CHURCH'S EPIC POTENTIAL

Reconciling the

generations in the church would breathe new life into a faltering institution and perhaps even save civilization.

On its face, this claim seems far-fetched. But as someone who has invested his whole life working with young adults, I am more convinced every day that it is true. The gap between generations is killing the church, and we desperately need to have a conversation about it. There has never in history been greater opportunity for the church to truly influence culture, and we are on the verge of missing it.

This is a short book, so it won't take long for you to decide whether or not you agree. What will take longer is deciding what to do in response. In the end, that's all that really matters.

As we consider the role of different generations in the church, and the church in the culture, I will introduce you to many people whose grasp (or ignorance) of the core truths I'll discuss affected the very course of history, underscoring how momentous is the crisis, and yet how great the opportunity, that lies before us.

*****

London, England, 2012

The library at Westminster Abbey is not open to the public, which makes visiting it feel like being invited into an exclusive time warp, with modern computer technology set in rooms adorned with ancient beams and saggy shelves stuffed with volumes whose pages were once turned by kings and queens of old. Even a couple of hours there makes one feel somehow smarter and more attached to the important events of the past, like gazing into the eyes of history itself.

But at some point in my visit, I happened to glance at my watch. The Abbey was closing for the day, and there was still one more monument I wanted to see.

A few minutes later, thanks to a well-placed telephone call from one of the librarians, I was being ushered past the guards, upstream from the crowds pouring out of the Abbey, and into a side alcove featuring a tiny monument, easily overlooked, celebrating the life and achievements of William Wilberforce. Wilberforce, as the movie *Amazing Grace* made people aware, was a tireless opponent of the trans-Atlantic slave trade and champion of efforts to revive England in a time of decadence and cruelty.

Amidst the fading echoes of the day's last departing guests, I stood reading the inscription on the Wilberforce monument. Suddenly my eyes stopped on a stunning phrase in the paragraph chiseled into the base. As if by heavenly decree, the swelling of organ music

"In the first 100 years of the church, there were only 25,000 believers. In the next 200 years, it went from 25,000 to 20 million believers. What happened? A man came onto the scene. He uttered three words to change it all. He said: believe (what you believe is important), behave (how you live is important) and belong (relationships are critical)."

—Josh McDowell
Quoted From Grow Together Film

announcing Evensong sent a chill through my body and carried its profound message into my soul.

Suddenly my path in life was clearer than it had ever been before.

*****

Rome, circa
AD 100

Mathetes took in the whole scene with wide-eyed wonder; wide-eyed partly because of the dimly lit underground room but mostly because he could hardly believe what was taking place in front of him.

The singing and rituals were unfamiliar to Mathetes. He wasn't sure he believed what they were singing about, but somehow the people trusted him anyway and allowed him into their assembly. He admired these brave souls. They abided by laws that treated them unjustly. They suffered persecution. They returned insult with honor, and punishment with good works.

But what Mathetes saw was completely unlike the religious ceremonies offering tribute to the Roman gods. It was so … understated. And yet so natural.

Mathetes knew that something about this simple gathering would change the world and that Rome, with all its history, all its philosophy and all its power, could do nothing to stop it.

*****

Willemstad, the Netherlands,
1953

The levees were everything. If they did not hold, hundreds of people would be dead by morning. And the reports of this storm worried Cor van der Hooft, mayor of the village of Willemstad.

Van der Hooft paced back and forth. All evening, gale force winds had sent the spring tide crashing dangerously into fragile levees. Surely they would collapse. And yet even the provincial commissioner had returned to bed after national officials assured him all was well.

Considering his options, van der Hooft became agitated. How could he face his children, his grandchildren and neighbors if he did not warn them? How would he respond to the accusing question: "You knew this was coming and you said nothing?"

"And yet if I'm wrong," he muttered to himself, "I will look like an absolute fool by morning."

Van der Hooft had already taken the step of organizing citizens to go door to door. How was their message being received? Suddenly there was a brief knock and then a loud crash as the door flew open, spilling in rain and a breathless member of the warning party: "Mayor! They aren't listening to us!"

Life and death were in his hands. Suddenly Cor van der Hooft knew exactly what to do.

*****

Detroit, Michigan, 1957

"Well boys, it's over."

Nobody said a word. The occasional puff of a cigarette kept the smoke circulating among the boardroom's occupants. The assembled men absorbed the news; their long, hard fight to save the company had failed. The Packard Motor Car Company — the glory of the automotive age — was no more.

Packard's demise became inevitable in 1937 with a decision that seemed like a stroke of genius at the time. As one year passed into another, though, the deadliness of this decision became ever clearer. Only the burial remained.

The restless men in shirtsleeves and ties rocked back and forth around the table as the chairman droned on about saving the company's famous name through a merger with Studebaker.

No one heard him. Their minds were already racing ahead to the mocking words they know would appear the next morning in the Detroit News. Packard's simple, confident advertising slogan would now be the butt of jokes: "Ask the man who owns one." No one was buying Packards anymore, so there was no one left to ask.

*****

San Francisco, California, 1978

Aaron gazed around the room as the leader, who had introduced himself as Phil, stuffed marshmallow after marshmallow in his cheeks and tried talking, to peals of laughter from the children.

Phil was unlike anyone Aaron had ever met in his native South Korea. A pale, lanky man in his early 30s, with thinning red hair and a shrill voice, Phil was not a commanding presence. And yet in his big-hearted way, he made everything fun, whether group hikes, driving the church bus or making a 10-foot-long banana split.

Aaron was wary; Phil took Christianity way too seriously, he thought. Phil's knack for turning everyday moments into thought-provoking conversations about spiritual things was, well, weird. At least it seemed that way for a foreigner learning the language and facing the daily dangers of a low-income housing project.

On the brink of his teenage years, Aaron was conflicted. Going to church was fun, but he had big questions in his agile mind about music and art and books. Would Phil's Christianity have anything to say about these? Aaron decided to ask. To this day, he remains surprised at how the resulting conversation — conversations, plural — changed the course of his life.

*****

Manitou Springs, Colorado, 1983

As the station wagon glided up the street, the young man glanced out the window at the imposing antique hotel before him. Yellow with brown trim. Must have had a sale on ugly paint. But hey, he was fresh out of high school, ready for an adventure, and his parents were dropping him off for two weeks. It was Colorado. What could be so bad about that?

As the boy lugged his suitcase into the dimly lit lobby, he came face to face with a tall, muscular man sporting a summer tan and balding head. "Welcome to Summit," he said. "I'm Dave Noebel."

The young man couldn't help but stare at the man's absurdly large, thick glasses. "I hear you have a lot of answers, which is good because I have a lot of questions," said the boy abruptly.

All he got in reply was a chuckle. And then the man said, "Fair enough. But first, I have a question for you."

*****

History is a river, drawing together great happenings with small ones, swirling their individual molecules together until their separate actions seemingly create one motion. What we do as individuals is both irrelevant in the larger sweep of things and at the same time irreplaceable. Within time's unyielding banks, we are both being carried along and altering history's course through the choices we make.

This is a book about those decisions and choices — all quadrillion or so of them made every day by billions of people — and how they might be made differently in a way that could change the course of history.

As we learn to decide differently about how we relate across generations, success is not guaranteed, nor is failure inevitable. Yet whether we change course and flourish is not a decision of individual wills. We must *together* decide, because at the center of our choosing is not a solitary soul but a body — an institution given by God. It's called the church.

To people with a small view of church, who think church is a place we go or a duty we fulfill, it is absurd to claim that church can change society. Those with eyes to see, though, will glimpse something beyond the ritualized performance to which we have become accustomed, to a fuller reality of how church transforms human relationships and can lead to an extraordinary transformation of society.

A small view of church is nothing new. In his letter to the church at Ephesus, the Apostle Paul speaks of a divide between the "circumcised" and "uncircumcised" that is killing the church.

I've asked many pastors about this. "Who are the circumcised and uncircumcised today?"

"Well, it's the churched and the unchurched," many say.

But Paul is not talking about those who do not yet believe. He's talking about people who are in church but feel *out* of it. The other day, I asked some of my younger staff members at Summit Ministries about where they see the dividing line between the "circumcised" and "uncircumcised" today. They said, "Maybe the dividing line is between the older and younger generations."

"Why do you say that?" I asked.

"Because each generation has its idea of what church is — what it looks like and what happens there — and our generation just isn't interested in following arbitrary cultural rules that make church meaningful to a few but squeeze the rest of us out."

Exactly.

The greatest cultural divide in the church is not between the rich and poor or between majority and minority cultures. It is a generational divide: silent, invisible, culturally-acceptable segregation by age.

If this is true, even remotely so, we ought to heed Paul's proc-
lamation of Christ as the only one by which the dividing wall of
hostility between the in-group and the out-group is abolished and
unity is restored.

Generational divides kill churches. But reuniting the generations is possible, and it makes probable dramatic change that can
revitalize the spread of the gospel and display God's glory in a way
that whole nations will praise him.

To grasp this vision, though, we must release a catastrophic,
nearly unavoidable assumption. If we don't figure out what this error
is and how to reverse course, three generations hence our progeny
will be powerless to reverse its effects.

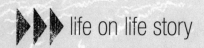 life on life story

Casual Mentoring

I've often thought of mentoring as something for professionals only — people like counselors who are trained to mentor. Recent comments from three people — all in their mid-30s — have proven me wrong.

The first came from a co-worker when I was transitioning to a new job. A few days before leaving my old company, he came into my office and thanked me for the example I'd been to him. He said he considered me one of his closest mentors and would always remember me as such. Strange, because I never sought this position or spent extra time with him after work. I just recall being there for him when he needed input, which was only on an occasional basis.

Shortly thereafter, I had two similar comments from men at my church. Due to death and relocation, the first young man had lost contact with some of his mentors. He told me that I came into his life at the right time to fill that gap. Again, very strange, because I never spent time with him outside of church. I simply took the time to listen to him after services. He liked to talk, so it often meant we were the last ones in the building.

The third comment came from a fellow member of our church leadership team. It was at my last meeting as a member a few weeks before I was moving to another state. He also shared that I'd been a true mentor to him as a father. He — like me — had three daughters. Mine were now adults while his were still small. As with the other two men, I never spent time conscientiously attempting to be his mentor. My wife and I had simply showed an interest in his family and spoken with them at church.

I know there's definitely more to mentoring than what I did with these men. But I also realize that just being a godly example and showing genuine interest in others leads to mentoring by default.

This is something anyone can do. Don't underestimate the power of caring for people in your everyday life.

—David

2

A CATASTROPHIC ASSUMPTION AND THE METAPHOR THAT REDEEMS IT

The crisis facing

the church is a generational one: The baton is not being successfully passed to those who would secure the church's influence for good in the coming years. Nothing illustrates the reasons for this crisis more than the demise of one of America's once great companies. Here's the story.

At the corner of East Grand Boulevard and Concord Street in Detroit stands the world's largest abandoned building — 3.5 million square feet, big enough to accommodate 68 football fields. Once a thriving factory, it now symbolizes what happens when a company forsakes the source of its greatness.

The ruins are the former home of the Packard Motor Car Company, which was created at the close of the 19th century by James

Ward Packard, whose complaints about his recently purchased Winton automobile led an exasperated Mr. Winton to huff, "If you don't like my car, build a better one."

Packard did just that. Indeed, within four years the Packard Motor Car Company had become known as America's luxury automobile manufacturer. Packards were expensive. While the 1903 Ford Model T ("any color you want, as long as it's black") sold for $375, 1903 Packards *started* at $2,600. In today's dollars, that would get you a brand new Cadillac Escalade and a year's worth of gas. And that was Packard's *entry-level* car.

By inventing the American luxury automobile, Packard created a formidable brand ensuring 30 years of enviable reputation and profits. Even during the Great Depression, Packard continued producing luxury cars and became one of America's few successful companies. But then it made a fatal mistake.

In 1937, Packard's management decided it didn't want to make the *best* cars anymore — it wanted to make the *most* cars. The Packard team engineered an affordable economy model. Sales soared. Profits grew. Packard even added to its base by producing airplane engines during World War II. Things were going brilliantly.

At the war's end, though, Packard's military contracts dissolved. Desperate, its executives tried reclaiming its luxury reputation. Unfortunately, people no longer saw Packard that way. Its once-envied design lines now seemed quaint. The luster of Packard's brand was gone.

Packard was flush with enough cash to hang on for many more years. But today, Packard's factory features only crumbling cement, broken windows and spray-painted gang symbols. The glory of the Packard Motor Car Company has departed. What happened?

The Packard company died in the service of a false premise: More is better. Packard measured success wrongly. By focusing on the number of cars produced rather than its brand strength, it lost both.

"At this point it's anyone's guess whether these kids who are walking away from their faith are going to come back. I haven't seen it yet. ... You can't necessarily point fingers and assign complete blame, but something seems to be missing."

—Alex Harris

Quoted From Grow Together Film

The undisciplined pursuit of more has destroyed many a company. It has also destroyed many a church. The church in America is hemorrhaging, and if present trends continue, it could soon lose much of what remains of its membership. Even more tragically, it could lose its unique position as a beacon for what is right and true in a nation that is in cultural collapse.

Can the church can learn something from the Packard error before it is too late?

How the Church's Success Led to Its Decline

Evangelical Christianity arose in 20th-century America as a response to mainline churches' abandonment of basic biblical doctrines such as the bodily resurrection of Christ. Contrary to what we're often told, evangelicalism was not a rural movement, nor was it a conservative political one. If anything, it was a populist movement that all — young and old, Democrat and Republican, urban and rural — embraced. It became one of the most successful movements of any kind, in any nation, in history.[1]

For example, in 1942 and 1943, more people listened to evangelical preacher Charles Fuller's *Old-Fashioned Revival Hour* than any other radio program.[2] Evangelistic crusades in the last half of the 20th century brought millions of people to make decisions for Christ. Many of these converts went into missions in order to spread the evangelical message around the world. Evangelicalism's growth seemed unstoppable.

At some point, and no one knows exactly when, evangelicalism in America plateaued and began to decline. In 2009, a respected blogger named Michael Spencer wrote an essay on "The Coming Evangelical Collapse," in which he gloomily predicted that "the end of evangelicalism as we know it is close."[3]

Win Arn, founder of Church Growth, Inc., claims that out of the 350,000 churches in America, four out of five have plateaued or are declining. Around 3,500 to 4,000 churches close their doors every year, he calculates.[4] With more than 200 million non-church-goers, America now ranks in the top four least-churched nations in the world.

It's worst among the young. Researcher Ed Stetzer found that of those who regularly attended youth group as teens, only about 30 percent continue regular church attendance as 20-somethings.[5] A lower percentage of Millennials attend church than any previous generation in American history.[6] Today the rising generation is called the "Nones," as in, "What is your religious preference?" "None."

This is *reverse* conversion. It's not merely failure to reach those who have never darkened a church door; it's an exodus of those we thought were the church's shining lights. They came, they saw, they bought; now they're asking for a refund.

And yet, the rising generation leaving the church isn't the worst of it. We're actually facing a much bigger problem.

Empty Lives, Not Just Empty Pews

Refusing to go to church and forsaking a biblical worldview are symptoms of a larger disease: purposelessness. Stanford University professor William Damon says that only one in five young people ages 12 to 22 say they know where they want to go, what they want to accomplish in life, and why.[7] This is not a generation that is temporarily disoriented on the way to its destination; it's a generation that *has* no destination.

What we used to describe as a mid-life crisis is pushing downward through the lifespan. In his song "Why Georgia?" singer/

"We're at risk
of losing
an entire
generation."

—Stuart Briscoe
Quoted From Grow Together Film

songwriter John Mayer wonders about "the outcome of a still verdictless life" and muses:

> I rent a room and I fill the spaces with
> Wood in places to make it feel like home,
> But all I feel's alone.
> It might be a quarter life crisis
> Or just the stirring in my soul.[8]

Picked up by sociologists, the term "quarter-life crisis" captures the fear and confusion of young adults who've lost the plot. They're 25 and tired of church. That's a problem. But the bigger problem is that they're 25 and tired of *life* and they do not believe the recovery of meaning goes through the church.

The church could offer a vision, some compelling future to work toward. But most churches don't. One student in my college class put it this way: "Dr. Myers, I've gone to the same church my whole life. There are people who have attended there for 40 years, and it has made absolutely no difference in their lives. Why should I keep going?"

I couldn't answer because I knew that this young man was surrounded by people who populated the church pews out of habit rather than a desire for personal and social transformation. Such people may appear to be together, but they're actually distant. Their nearness is compartmentalized, much like the citizens of the Gray City in C.S. Lewis' *The Great Divorce*, where with each passing year, people separated further from meaning, and thus from one another. Lewis' vision is not one of heaven; it's a picture of hell.

People who sense a separation of church and meaning usually do not realize that our acceptance of this separation isn't merely a matter of neglect. It is part of a very well-conceived plan hatched in the revolutionary fervor of Europe more than 250 years ago.

The Enlightenment Plan to Rob the Church of Meaning

In 1751, French philosopher Denis Diderot began compiling his *Encyclopédie* as a means of organizing all of human knowledge. Ultimately Diderot's work contained 71,818 articles on every imaginable subject. The goal: enlightenment.

Enlightenment, Diderot believed, happens when people abandon superstitious God-belief and make humanity the measure of all things. "For man is the unique starting point," he said, "and the end to which everything must finally be related if one wishes to please, to instruct, to move to sympathy, even in the most arid matters and in the driest details."[9]

Through the influence of Diderot, Voltaire, Rousseau and others, *knowledge* replaced *wisdom* as the highest good.[10] Today most people see the two as indistinguishable. This is a problem. While knowledge and wisdom start from the same place, they arrive at utterly different destinations.

Knowledge is individually held; wisdom is a community good — one can only be wise in relation to other people. Knowledge becomes more valuable the more of it you have; wisdom's value is in *quality*, not quantity. Knowledge catalogs humanity's choices; wisdom measures the flow of those choices as they pour into history. Knowledge can isolate and track individual actions, but wisdom is more interested in their *interaction*. Knowledge can be used equally well for evil purposes as for pure ones, but wisdom inherently operates in the service of the good. As the philosopher Mortimer Adler put it, "To act wisely is to act well, even as to have wisdom is to use it."[11]

There's more. Wisdom breathes life into others. Knowledge, on the other hand, holds in its own air, inflating its holders until they believe they are bigger than they actually are. This was Diderot's problem. In his boundless drive for radical autonomy and freedom, Diderot rejected all authority but his own. "Man will never be free until the last king is strangled with the entrails of the last priest," he said.[12]

The children born of the union of wisdom and knowledge were the true children of light: medicine, science, invention, economic growth and industrialization. This light spread around the world, amassing an unprecedented amount of economic and social capital and advancing civilization more in 200 years than in the previous 5,000.

Knowledge by itself, though, produced illegitimate offspring: colonialism, Marxism, fascism, cronyism. Masked in beneficence, these wanton ideas acted with shocking brutality, bludgeoning their way across the face of the earth and causing more bloodshed in those 200 years than in all of human history combined.

These days, knowledge is still on the throne. Any wisdom that the church can offer now is spurned as quaint and irrelevant. Church is something one "goes" to out of shame or duty, or for networking or entertainment purposes, not a place where people may find timeless truths and sinners may drink of the living water and be rejuvenated.

It's not just the culture's fault. The vision of church as an oasis of transformation in the desert of vulgarity has been abandoned by many in the church itself. Culture is too far gone, the thinking goes. But in saying this, we aren't speaking the truth as much as we are showing how thick the poison of hopelessness runs in our veins, numbing our limbs and making listlessness seem normal.

In our parched state, there is good news; very, very good news. A wedding invitation has been issued. Turns out, the kingdom of heaven is a bridal proposal to be accepted, not an edifice to be built.

In the end, the stilted enlightenment vocabulary of knowledge-over-wisdom is too impoverished to describe how stunning the bridegroom's arrival actually is. We hear talk of decline, despair and decimation, but at a wedding feast, such words wilt in the face of joyful words like redemption, restoration and reconciliation.

It may seem an odd place to begin, but to reclaim the greatness of the church of Jesus Christ, we need new words crafted in the fullness of wisdom — new metaphors, new analogies, and new ways to think and speak and conceive of life in the light of *Imago Dei*. We need to restore very old ways of speaking and realize their power anew. Frankly, we need to rebel against mere knowledge and embrace the kind of wisdom that inspires generations to reunite around their culture-shaping potential.

Rebel Metaphors

Metaphors matter. For example, thinking of people as machines leads us to wrongly conceive of humanity as that which can be programmed, controlled, tinkered with, organized, and, as the definition of manufacturing states, produced "mechanically without inspiration or originality."[13]

"More is better" makes perfect sense for machines. A machine bottling 200 soft drinks an hour is *better* than one bottling 50. A car tuned to produce more horsepower on less fuel is better than one not so tuned. But for what matters most about people, more is not better.

The deepest and most enduring metaphors for humanity, those that represent what is truly better, are of the earth. They are nuanced and humble, yet gracefully powerful. Fruitfulness rather than productivity. Cultivation rather than manufacturing. Abundance rather than stockpiling. Seeds rather than parts.

To "seed" something is to put it in fertile soil. The metaphor is everywhere in the Bible, referring to everything from plants to people to nations to prophesies about the coming Messiah. The metaphors of soil, ground, fruit, watering, tilling, farming, pruning, nourishing, gardening, harvesting, laboring and even enjoying the fruit of one's labors in the earth — eating, drinking and resting — are found on nearly every page.

Metaphors about cultivating describe what actually sustains life. Our food doesn't come from factories, it comes from the earth. Someone, somewhere, worked hard for it — planting, watering, tilling, harvesting, sorting, shipping, mixing, cooking. We may let our manufacturing metaphor trick us into forgetting where things come from, into thinking in terms of a division of labor or efficiency. But without agriculture, human life is impossible.

The same is true in uniting the church across generations. When we use the right metaphors, we can better glimpse the abundance God truly wants us to have. We *will* have more. But it will be a much better "more," a flourishing in a world teeming with life. It is a *meaningful* more. In the Hebrew of Genesis 1:31, it is the "very good," the "*towb meod.*" It is exceedingly, abundantly, richly, immeasurably good in a festive, generous, intelligent, charming, splendid way.

It's a radical shift to see ourselves as more like grains of wheat or branches on a vine than toasters or smart phones. We are not engineers seeking efficiency or predictability or a lower error rate. We are cultivators with the power to nurture, seek the goodwill of, tend and prepare others to bear fruit.

As we will see, this change of language — and all it represents — just might save civilization.

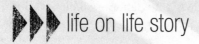 life on life story

Empowering the Poor

Kit Danley found her life purpose in college — caring for the poor. For more than 40 years she has been a mother figure and mentor to thousands of inner city children and their families through Neighborhood Ministries, which she helped start in 1982.

Like a lot of kids in the early '70s, I wanted to find meaning in life. I started Bible studies and began sharing my faith. I got involved with a group called Campus Ambassadors. We were mentored by incredible people like Vernon Grounds, Rufus Jones and Don Davis. I learned about God's heart for the poor, which became evident as I discovered there are over 400 passages and more than 1,000 verses dealing with the poor in Scripture.

At Neighborhood Ministries, we don't give up on throwaway kids, the ones that most people have decided aren't worth the effort. We aggressively intervene when kids are trapped in self-destructive behaviors. Our programs become refuges for children and teens from the horrors of drive-by shootings, drugs, street life and the instability that's so common in their lives.

We invest in long-term relationships. We stay involved in people's lives for as long as they allow us to. We track transient families, encouraging them to stay involved in our programs. Our tutoring, mentoring, jail visitation and biblical counseling give them the help they need to survive and succeed.

A big part of our calling is to mentor indigenous leaders. Through faithful friendships over the long haul, we help people discover and develop their God-given gifts and abilities. We emphasize character development and servant leadership. One thing we won't do is patronize. We don't want to be a disempowering organization, one that creates more dependency among the poor.

—Kit

3

HOW THE CHURCH SAVES CIVILIZATION

Comrade Ivan's words

were whipping the crowd into a revolutionary fervor while the Czar's police stood on the outskirts of the mob, fidgeting nervously. Suddenly the police captain barked a command, troops rushed in and all hell broke loose. The assembled laborers exploded in anger, determined never again to submit to the Czar's abuse. Every drop of blood drawn by lash or sword was paid for by another drawn with a fist. When the dust settled, several people were dead and dozens more were injured.

Friends helped Comrade Ivan — so nicknamed to defray suspicion — to escape. Soon, though, the Czar's forces discovered who he was: Pitirim Sorokin. Imprisoned on six different occasions, Sorokin became a revolutionary hero.

October 1917, the Bolsheviks seized control of the Russian government and began savagely exacting retribution, even murdering the Czar and his family in cold blood. It dawned on Sorokin, to his horror, that his Bolshevik brethren were just as brutal and mindless as the oppressors from whose shackles they had been freed. He criticized them openly, for which he was branded a counter-revolutionary and hunted. To protect his family, Sorokin turned himself in and was sentenced to die.

Amazingly, the execution order never came. On December 12, 1918, Sorokin was released from prison on direct orders from Lenin. One of Sorokin's former students, now a Commissar, had persuaded Lenin to release Sorokin and court his allegiance instead of killing him.

Thus began an uneasy truce that ended in 1922 when, faced with banishment, Sorokin and his wife obtained passports and immigrated to the United States. Upon his arrival, Sorokin embarked on an astounding career as a sociologist, first at the University of Minnesota and then at Harvard, authoring a colossal body of work on social crisis and the birth and death of civilization. It was in this work that he discovered something many academics find infuriating, but which at the same time inspires hope for civilization.

How New Civilizations Are Born From the Death of the Old

Having had a front row seat to the Bolshevik revolution, Sorokin had seen first-hand how an ancient and seemingly robust civilization could collapse overnight. Barbarians cannot destroy from without that which has not already been hollowed out from within. When the culture-creators and maintainers lose the will to preserve civilization, Sorokin knew, it is time to write its obituary.

From Sorokin's perspective, the West was in as much danger as those nations succumbing to the communist onslaught. He saw the West as bankrupt of truth and drunk on amusement and greed, lacking the will to preserve its founding principles. The gun at its head was held by its own hand. Sorokin called this kind of culture "sensate" and argued that all civilizations passed through such a stage just prior to their deaths.

Sorokin's analysis angered the cultural elite of his day who believed that infatuation with human-centered thinking and fleshly desire was a good thing. "We're not dead yet!" they cried.

But Sorokin did not believe sensate cultures ceased breathing immediately when the life support of their heritage was removed. With a sufficiently rich cultural inheritance, they can live on for decades. But like a consumer abusing his debit card, sensate cultures inevitably get an "insufficient funds" notice. And when they do, the collapse can be sudden.

Unlike the pessimists who cry "The end is near," Sorokin went past the question of "How do civilizations die?" to a more important question: "What happens *after* civilizations die?" His answer was, and still is, shocking. People weary of a sensate culture's banality often return to transcendent truth, forming a new "ideational" civilization that rises like a phoenix out of the ashes, reinvigorating society, restoring human dignity and birthing civilization anew. On the other side of the invitation to a civilization's funeral is an invitation to another's christening.

The time of transition, Sorokin believed, would be brutal, with the sensate culture fighting with all its remaining strength against any sort of reformation or renaissance. But if the new civilization's will was strong enough, and rooted in what Sorokin called the "kingdom of God," it could transcend the "weary and torturing pilgrimage from calamity to calamity" and find the way of life even in the valley of death's shadow.

Sorokin published his findings in the 1950s. If he was correct, we are *right now* in the time of transition. We are free to choose our

"If the church really united
the generations within the
church and helped them to
see themselves as a team,
living together for the glory
of God, making their home
in reality an embassy of
the kingdom of God,
the salt and light impact
would explode."

–Gregg Harris
Quoted From Grow Together Film

course, but we must *choose* it rather than just endure it. As Sorokin phrased it, "the more unteachable we are, and the less freely and willingly we choose the sole course of salvation open to us, the more inexorable will be the coercion, the more pitiless the ordeal, the more terrible the *dies irae* [day of wrath] of the transition."[1]

Could our culture's impoverishment be, not the end of our civilization, but the birth of a new one? Of course. As I write we are seeing Christianity birthed in a whole new way in countries around the world. This conversion is so profound that, as sociologist Philip Jenkins notes, America and Africa could soon become the continents with the greatest number of Christians.[2]

But can "mere" religious conversion actually change civilization? You might be surprised at the answer.

What Civilization Is ...

In his 11-volume history of the West, Will Durant defines civilization as "social order promoting cultural creation." Civilizations, he says, have an economic system, a political structure, moral traditions, and a means of pursuing knowledge and the arts. Civilization, Durant wrote, "begins where chaos and insecurity end. For when fear is overcome, curiosity and constructiveness are free, and man passes by natural impulse toward the understanding and embellishment of life."[3]

Civilizations are living things and are like trees whose roots must be protected by the rich earth, fed by the sun and watered by the rains. They must be nourished and protected from the hacking, parching, crushing influence of barbarism. Otherwise the long hard slog of progress may be halted in just a moment of time. "From barbarism to civilization requires a century," Durant warned; "from civilization to barbarism needs but a day."[4]

What causes such destruction? Historian Christopher Dawson noted: "Barbarism is not a picturesque myth or a half-forgotten memory of a long-passed stage of history, but an ugly underlying reality which may erupt with shattering force whenever the moral authority of a civilization loses its control."[5]

... and How Christianity Saved It

In Western civilization, the moral authority to which Dawson refers is Christianity. French philosopher Luc Ferry, an atheist, says it was to Christianity that Western civilization "owed its entire democratic inheritance."[6] We often hear that democracy was birthed in Greece and Rome, but the fact is that Greece and Rome were haughty, elite-driven cultures with no respect for ordinary people.[7] Christianity assigned value to people previously considered expendable, including slaves, women and enemies.

And Christianity uniquely did this. Most worldviews are either *materialist*, believing only in the physical world, or *immaterialist*, believing the physical world is an illusion. Materialists have no logical reason for caring about anything "soulish" such as humans having inherent spiritual value. Immaterialists have no logical reason to care about improving things in this illusory world.

The Christian worldview transcends other worldviews' self-imposed boundaries, revealing instead an immaterial and transcendent God who, as Father, Son and Holy Spirit, exists in an eternal relationship *within himself.* This God, in turn, created the *material* world and made human beings not as slaves but as divinely equipped, breathed-into bearers of the *Imago Dei.*[8]

The Surprising Way the Church Influences Civilization

At the heart of Christianity, then, is relationship — not rules. Theologian Walter Kaiser says that the primary name by which he reveals himself in the Old Testament is Yahweh, which means "I am." As Kaiser puts it, he was "the God who would be dynamically, effectively present when he was needed and when men called on him."[9] This was not a static god about whom we tell outlandish stories, but a dynamic, active, involved, *personal* God.[10] God is, as D.A. Carson points out, "a talking God."[11]

Even our system of laws finds its basis in this understanding of God. God does not only speak to kings, Christian minister Samuel Rutherford argued in *Lex Rex*, but rather communicates his will to all of us. We all have the law written on our hearts.[12] John Locke made a similar argument in his *Two Treatises on Government.*[13] These two authors deeply influenced America's founders.

Historian Alvin Schmidt says that Christianity's teaching about the value of humans has positively influenced everything from the abolition of slavery, to the banning of child molestation, to freedom and dignity for women, to the formation of hospitals and schools, to the securing of liberty and justice for all, to the advancement of science, to the development of great art and architecture, to the sanctity of human life.[14] Sociologist Rodney Stark claims further that effective moral opposition to slavery arose *only* because of Christian theology.[15] Various cultures opposed slavery in certain circumstances or for themselves, but opposing slavery as sinful in all its forms was something only Christianity did.

The Christian doctrine of sin was of critical importance to the formation of our civilization because it focused on changing society for the better without forcing it into hopelessly utopian visions. The words used for sin imply losing one's way or straying from a path or a cracking of one's relationship with God.[16] Sin is not just "out there," but also "in here." Recognizing this, early Christians opposed utopian visions and promoted systems of accountability to forestall and curb the effects of evil and to champion justice and honesty.

Without people who think and live like Jesus, what we call civilization might not even exist. And the institution that through history has led people to Christian conviction and discipled them to live this way is the church. The church has the same effect on civilization that salt has on meat; it protects and preserves. It is the transmitter of moral conviction from one generation to the next.

Failure to pass on godly principles in one generation always leads to bloodshed in the next, whether at the hands of a tyrant like Hitler, who condemned those he wished were never born, or through the pens of Supreme Court justices whose signatures ensure that millions never will be. Where many men are soft, a few hard men will rule.

When the older generation loses the energy and the younger generation loses the will to preserve civilization, we can expect epic battles for basic liberties like freedom of religion and freedom of speech, and worse, rapid erosion of ethical norms. Chaos and insecurity re-emerge. Fear reigns. Creativity and constructiveness die. Civilization fades to a flicker with various forms of barbarism jostling one another for the chance to snuff it out entirely.

The real tragedy of the hemorrhaging of the church is not just the loss of members who teach Sunday school or tithe to pay for a building or salaries. It's what we lose when the wisdom of the older disconnects from the energy of the younger. Let's take a look at some specific examples of how this might be so.

Can the Church Really Make That Much Difference?

Some people doubt whether reconnecting the generations in the church would really make that much difference in the culture. As we saw earlier, three out of four young adults raised in the church disengage in their 20s.[17] Contemplate that statistic for a moment.

Picture in your mind eight adorable 5-year-olds sitting in a Sunday school classroom coloring pictures of Noah's Ark and singing "Jesus Loves Me." By the time they reach their 20s:

▶ Only two will still be involved in church.
▶ One or two will have become atheists.
▶ One will have converted to another religion such as Mormonism, Islam or Buddhism.
▶ One, possibly two, will return to church once they have children.
▶ The rest will have disappeared from the spiritual landscape entirely.

Right now there are about 20 million 20-somethings in America. Roughly one-third of them claim to be evangelical Christians, which is around 7 million people. If the statistic above is close to being accurate, *approximately 5.25 million of them are now uninvolved in church.*

What would happen if these 5.25 million truly experienced God relationally and became energized, spiritually mature, motivated young adults focused on the redemptive work of the church?

First, there would be incredible mentoring opportunities. Twenty-somethings make great mentors to youth because they're closer in age and have more free time. Mentoring could be a difference-maker for the approximately 5 million at-risk American youth who are headed toward lives of substance abuse and crime. Churches could lead this effort by pairing at-risk youth with 20-something mentors, accounting for every single one of them. Imagine millions of previously abandoned, rejected children finding love and community in the arms of the church and, ultimately, having the chance to embrace Christ!

Second, there would be increased family stability. Children of divorce are significantly more likely to be affected by poverty, drug use, suicide or crime. Although it's commonly thought that Christians parallel nonbelievers when it comes to divorce rates, sociologist Bradley Wright has shown that those who attend church regularly are significantly less likely to get divorced.[18] How many marriages of 20-somethings would be saved if millions more of them were engaged in church? Imagine the godly legacy that could be passed on and the stable society that could result!

Third, there would be virtually unlimited community outreach. The impact of 5.25 million people giving an hour a week to works of charity — something that churchgoers do in significantly higher percentages than non-churchgoers — would be enormous. This small weekly contribution would amount to the equivalent number of hours of 130,000 full-time social workers sharing compassion and helping people rebuild their lives. Imagine local communities never again lacking Christian volunteers motivated by the gospel!

Fourth, we would experience unheard-of ministry opportunities. If these 5.25 million 20-somethings tithed just 2 percent of an average income of $30,000 per year, it would raise an additional 3.15 billion dollars that could, for example, fund almost 300 new full-time missionaries in *each and every country in the world*. Imagine how such disciplers could multiply the work of Christ in every tongue, tribe and nation for decades to come.

And it's easy to imagine the other 60 million people who attend church every weekend being inspired by this. It could change a nation. There is no conceivable alternative to a deep commitment to reuniting the generations that could have even a fraction of the impact on the redemptive ministry of the church, and the church, in turn, on society.

Not only is there no alternative, but as we will see, only the uniting of the generations can truly satisfy what people hunger for the most: truth, identity and meaning.

Let's begin with the hunger for truth. Such a hunger isn't satisfied by an enlightenment focus on knowledge but by something the early church understood about the nature and character of God. Something that would overthrow Rome's pagan stranglehold on the world and prepare for the rise of Christendom.

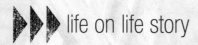 life on life story

Loving the Fatherless — and Their Mother

I was a single mother trying to raise a family in a new town when I met Mr. and Mrs. M. When Mrs. M. heard we needed to move a piano, she volunteered their help, and then she suggested we garden together over the summer. Soon we found ourselves spending day after dirty, sweaty day slowly getting acquainted in the garden. All the while I watched how Mrs. M. mothered her own children as well as mine — and wondered if I could trust these people.

My question was answered through how they cared for us. Only after several months of growing friendship did they even ask why I was raising my children alone. They happily watched my children without asking where I was going. This was a new experience; they trusted me! Frequently, they would invite us to church (where Mr. M. was the pastor), but I had been hurt by church in the past and politely refused.

This didn't change anything about how they treated us. Even when I hurt them, these people wouldn't get angry or defensive. Instead, they would quietly listen, ask questions, reflect on my concerns, calmly share truths from scripture and patiently trust my growth to God. I heard words like, "I'm sorry; I know this is hard for you." "You're hurting," and "I understand."

Over time, I learned what love looks like from Mr. and Mrs. M. Eventually, I agreed to visit their church and was astonished to find them to be the same people in church as they were while weeding the garden or fixing a lawnmower or disciplining children. I began to feel safe with God, His Word and His people again. I began to grow. My life and my family will never be the same because of their influence.

—Angela

4

THE
HUNGER
FOR
TRUTH

Mathetes sat quietly

in the darkened room, listening to soft conversations echoing faintly off the stone walls. He sensed that this ceremony, as simple as it was, would alter the course of history.

The service had started off fairly typically, as religious services go. Scriptures had been read, prayers offered. But what Mathetes found so unusual was how the worshipers were so *present* with one another, more like a *body* than a mob. There was no ecstasy or mindlessness. People were there to worship God, but *together*, not as individuals.

As Mathetes watched, initiates were paired with members to bounce ideas off one another in a ritual called "catechism." How very odd that the elders even cared what the initiates thought, patiently listening, answering questions. The word "catecheo," Mathetes knew, meant "to echo." As the conversations echoed, it became clear that initiates weren't just learning the universe's secrets. They were learning how to *live*.

What strange people, Mathetes thought, these *"atheists"* who openly rejected the pantheon of gods and insisted that One True God made everything and welcomed humanity into a personal relationship through his son, *Christos* the Messiah.

The odd gatherings had not escaped the notice of Rome's leading thinkers. Fierce debates broke out over how to handle the threat they posed: Christian teachings about serving rather than dictating, kindness rather than harshness, were thought to weaken Rome in the eyes of its ever-watchful enemies. They must be stopped. At least they would be easy to find. After all, their bizarre initiation rite of baptism was a public ritual; there were no secret followers.

Mathetes had seen Christian elders in the streets, initiates by their sides, conducting themselves with honor even when treated evilly by those who mistook their tenderness as weakness. Every day it became clearer that these were not weak people who worshiped death, but strong people who knew what it meant to really be alive.

Slipping quietly out of the gathering, Mathetes wandered the smoke and sewage-choked streets until he arrived at his humble dwelling. There, he took the ember plucked from the community fire, fanned his small lamp into flame, and began to write on a piece of parchment: "Dear Diognetus …"

*****

Mathetes' letter to Diognetus, the tutor of Marcus Aurelius and one of Rome's wisest and best thinkers, is now considered the earliest surviving apologetic for the Christian faith. The actual identity of Mathetes, which is the word for "disciple," is unknown. But his elegant description of Christianity's unpretentious goodness starkly contrasted with Rome's corruption: "They love all men, and are persecuted by all ... they are dishonored, and yet in their very dishonor are glorified."[1]

In the process of teaching an entirely new way to live, Christians redefined Rome's understanding of honor and glory. Honor and glory were due to *Christos*, not themselves, and a significant part of what honored and glorified Christos was the preparation of fully committed followers who would spread his message far and wide. In their book *The Unshakeable Truth*, Josh and Sean McDowell say that the early church's focus on *believing*, *behaving* and *belonging* caused a level of growth unprecedented in the history of religion — from 25,000 to 20 million believers in just 200 years.[2]

This could happen again, but we would first need to rethink our assumptions about how truth passes through the generations. For me, it is helpful to picture *truth* and *relationship* as two strands of a DNA double helix. If the strands are not coiled and bonded together, they can't reproduce. Truth without relationship leads to arrogance, while relationship without truth leads to apathy.

Let's take a look at how these strands coil together and what this might look like based on the generational cohorts alive today.

Truth Strand

Socrates said that the unexamined life is not worth living, but plenty of people live and die and seemingly examine very little. It's hard to get people to care about truth when thoughts about God, the world and human value seldom enter their consciousness. And yet each person hungers for truth. We want to know whether there is a good way to live each day and any principles that can help us find satisfaction in life, marriage, raising children, and being neighbors and citizens.

More and more people are grasping that Christianity forms a comprehensive worldview, a set of ideas, patterns, values and

"There's nothing
like one-on-one
influence. Show me
that you care, and
then I want to know
what you believe.
It doesn't usually
work the other
way around."

–James Dobson
Quote From Grow Together Interview

behaviors that encompass everything in the world.[3] Just as Jesus instructed his disciples to teach people to obey God in every area of life because "all authority in heaven and on earth" belongs to him (Matthew 28:18-20), we are to form, fill, create and *restore*, all in the authority of Christ.

But only half of today's pastors express confidence in the truth of basic Christian doctrines such as the accuracy of the Bible, Jesus' sinless nature, salvation by grace alone and the omnipotence of God. Untethered from these doctrines, Christianity stands mute in answer to life's ultimate questions. And pastoral uncertainties filter down; less than 10 percent of born-again Christians possess a Christian worldview.[4]

For professing Christians to reject a Christian worldview is to misunderstand faith itself. Faith is not faith because we have it but because the object of our faith is worthy, and worthiness can be objectively known, intellectually and emotionally, by a clear-eyed community of people. Such truth is rarely known *individually* (the word "idiot" comes from the Greek word for "one who alone knows").

Is it even possible to confidently know the truth beyond our own personal perspectives? Growing up as the son of evangelist Josh McDowell, Sean McDowell is comfortable discussing truth. As a college professor, though, Sean has noticed that most people doubt that spiritual knowledge is really knowable. "Imagine two kids taking a test," says McDowell. "One thinks he knows the right answer but isn't sure. The other actually knows the answer. The first student might get it right, but the second student is the one who will be able to make a coherent argument if he is challenged. That's what we need today."[5]

Being part of a truth-soaked, robustly thoughtful community is necessary but not sufficient. Truth apart from relationship says, "I know the truth. If you knew what I know, you would be better off."

The antidote to such arrogance is humility, which says, "I am so confident of this truth that I want to walk alongside you as God reveals it to you and confirms it to me." The answer to certainty without humility is not humility without certainty. It is certainty *with* humility.[6] This requires *understanding*, and that's where relationship comes in.

Relationship
Strand

Everyday truths such as how to prepare lemongrass chicken or which freeways to avoid during rush hour can be passed on en masse. But Capital-T Truth — life-altering, world-changing truth — only takes hold through relationship. Up to 75 percent of the people leaving church say they don't feel they belong.[7] It's a failure of the relationship strand, not the truth strand.

Truth intertwined with relationship says, "I can see where you're coming from, and I believe we can both grow by sharing our experiences." That's what the early church did. Mature believers patiently walked with young believers. Teachers were both teacher and student; students were both student and teacher. Monocular became binocular as they together glimpsed the vista of the virtuous life.

Relationship is the normal pattern in scripture for passing on truth. Joshua had Moses, Timothy had Paul, Isaac had Abraham, Ruth had Naomi, Elisha had Elijah. The Apostle Paul urged that faithful men be equipped to train faithful men, who would in turn be equipped to teach others (2 Timothy 2:2). This life-on-life method was seen as vital for keeping sound doctrine (Titus 2).

Knowing stuff doesn't make people good; in fact, it can puff people up (1 Corinthians 8:1).[8] And yet, we *can* know real things about God (2 Corinthians 10:5). Even while warning of its abuse, scripture elevates knowledge as a virtue. Intelligent, wise people seek it (Proverbs 18:15), and a lack of it destroys us (Hosea 4:6). We are not, as Pierre de Chardin claimed, "spiritual beings having human experiences."[9] We were meant to be knowers in a world that is meant to be known.

As we saw in chapter two, knowledge without wisdom is dangerous. But this is not to say that knowledge is bad. Without knowledge, people can't see Christianity's truth. Yet without relationship — the incarnation of wisdom and knowledge — people don't see the *point* of that truth.

With today's rapid changes, though, our experience with truth can be quite different depending on a factor people might not have even grasped in previous centuries: the year in which we were born.

Different Generations Experience Truth Differently

As we have seen, the last 200 years have brought more cultural and technological change than the previous 5,000 years combined.[10] Today, the pace of change is so fast that one generation's experiences in the world can be radically different from the experiences of those born just 20 years earlier.

On the one hand, we shouldn't make too much of the differences between generations. Our common humanity, shared experiences and similar cultural pressures surely outweigh our differences. But people's *experiences* in life seem to be significantly different depending on the era in which they were born, and it's hard for generations to see this about one another.

In the workplace, 65 percent of research respondents indicated that generation gaps make it hard to get things done. Many of the problems we thought were related to the loss of employee loyalty and work ethic are actually generational.[11]

Generational differences affect the church as well. Just by looking at the characteristics of various generational cohorts, we can probably figure out how this is so.

Traditionalists: born between 1925 and 1945, number 38 million in the U.S. Sometimes called "the Greatest Generation" for their survival of the Great Depression and feats of bravery in World War II and Korea, this generation is thought of as patriotic, conservative, hard-working and opinionated. Traditionalists go to church out of, well, tradition. It's a duty, and a welcome one.

Baby Boomers: born between 1946 and 1964, number 78 million in the U.S. This is the generation of Woodstock and Vietnam, of social unrest, racial conflict and massive, rapid technological change. Boomers are thought of as idealistic, yet also materialistic and focused on personal fulfillment. They walked away from church in a search for personal freedom, but found such freedom to be its own form of bondage. A surprising number returned to find the meaning they had been searching for all along.

Gen Xers: born between 1965 and 1979, number about 62 million in the U.S. Corporate and political scandals, the AIDS epidemic, and economic malaise have made them leery about so-called "progress." T.S. Eliot's plaintive refrain, "Where is the Life we have lost in living? ... Where is the knowledge we have lost in information?" echoes true for them. Seen as cynical and distrustful, but also entrepreneurial and self-reliant, Gen Xers who attend church are seeking refuge from a world of empty promises.

Millennials or Gen Yers: born between 1980 and 2001, number 92 million in the U.S. Millennials are viewed as entitled and impatient but also as team-minded and focused on work/life balance. And yet Millennials struggle more with moral issues. Young adults today are nine times more likely than Baby Boomers to engage in promiscuous sex, three times more likely to get drunk, and twice as likely to view pornography.[12] Millennials look for meaning in friendship. If church is not a source of friendship, they probably won't show up.

Gen Zers: born after 2001, are still in formation. It's hard to know exactly what will characterize this generational cohort. Some call them the "homeland" generation because their birth in the post-9/11 world, typified by constant war and economic sluggishness, offers little hope of the American Dream. They'd rather stay home than go out and take chances. Gen Zers seem simultaneously more connected and more isolated than any previous generation. Now they are discovering along with the rest of us that technology can make you laugh or cry, but it can't laugh or cry with you.[13]

As each generation lives out its lifespan, minutes turn into moments, moments into trends, and trends into epochs. But changes from generation to generation disguise the fact that we all have the same problem, and if we don't grapple with it, there's no chance of recovering a grand vision for the church.

Is Each Generation Becoming More Selfish?

It is a popular nostrum that each passing generation is more self-focused than the previous one. There is some truth to it. David Kinnaman and Gabe Lyons report: for the rising generation, priorities like wealth and personal fame easily trump priorities like being a leader in the community or becoming more spiritual.[14] A recent survey of British youth found that on a "very best thing in the world" top-10 list, "being a celebrity" was first and "God" was last.[15] Sociologist Christian Smith calls Millennials "Moralistic Therapeutic Deists"[16] whose deepest spiritual thought is "God loves me and wants me to be happy."[17]

But no one seems to be asking whether these trends are just taking place among the young. It could easily be the case that we're *all* getting worse but only the younger generation is being honest about it. Or it could be that the shortcomings in other generations are partly to blame. Some studies show that adolescents spent only about 5 percent of their time with their parents and only about 2 percent with other adults. Because of

this abandonment, Chap Clark points out, "the adolescent journey is lengthened, because no one is available to help move the
developmental process along."[18]

Whatever the reason, it seems that everyone — regardless of
generation — has quit asking, "What is right and how do I bring
myself to do it?" Instead they are asking, "What is good and how do
I get more of it *for* myself?" People no longer do things *just because
they're supposed to*. "Supposed to" is rarely even a category of meaning. People may *choose* to go to church, but they feel no obligation to
do so any more than they feel obligated to eat at a certain restaurant
because it's what granddad would have done.

Trying to win converts to Christianity by making "church duty"
more pleasant doesn't seem to be working. It leads only to what
Kenda Creasy Dean describes as "a low-commitment, compartmentalized set of attitudes aimed at 'meeting my needs' and 'making
me happy' rather than bending my life into a pattern of love and
obedience to God."[19]

If we are to recover the enthusiasm and rapid growth of the early
church, we'll have to do something entirely different.

What Shall We Do?

Doing our Christian duty during our own lifetimes is not enough. A
biblical cautionary tale about this is of the righteous king Hezekiah.
Hezekiah saw God utterly defeat an overwhelming enemy, but then
he traded his nation's future for a few more years of life (2 Kings
20). The moment Hezekiah's blood stopped pumping, the blood of
his subjects began flowing at the hands of his brutal son, Manasseh
(2 Kings 21).

There is no righteousness that does not include investing in
future generations. People who have figured this out have literally

changed the world — and not just in first-century Rome. Consider these examples:

▶ In the 400s, a man named Germanus discipled an escaped slave named Patrick, who then brought the gospel — and literacy — to remote Ireland even as Europe was being overrun by barbarians. By his early 20s, Patrick had prepared Ireland to replant the seeds of civilization across Europe.[20]

▶ Solomon Stoddard discipled his grandson Jonathan Edwards. Edwards was just 32 years old at the dawn of the Great Awakening that saw the conversion of 50,000 people in the American colonies and prepared the way for a new birth of freedom.[21]

▶ A New England minister named Jonathan Dickinson took under his wing a young man named David Brainerd who had been kicked out of Yale for being "overzealous" for Christ. At age 23, Brainerd become a missionary to the North American Indians and saw entire native communities changed by the gospel's power.[22]

▶ James Vinter, director of the lay preacher's association in Cambridge, England, saw a preaching gift in a teenager named Charles Haddon Spurgeon and assigned him to preach to gatherings of farm laborers. By age 25, Spurgeon was preaching to huge crowds, and thousands were converted.[23]

In each of these cases, someone put life-on-life influence with the rising generation ahead of their own advancement. And in each case, it was the relationship between the two that cemented each participant's sense of mission. This also satisfied another of the three great hungers everyone experiences: the hunger for an answer to the question "Who am I?" This is the hunger for identity.

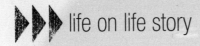 life on life story

Walking Through the Valley

My freshman year at Christian college, I was still adjusting to life in the U.S. after my family fled the civil war in Zimbabwe. I was grieving the loss of friends and was very unsure of my own identity. A college professor, Dr. D., and his wife, reached out to me. They believed in me and spoke blessings to me. I will never forget their words. But the greater lesson would be learned as we witnessed the D. family face their greatest trial.

Dr. and Mrs. D. and their four children lived near the dorms and truly felt like family. When their beautiful 12-year-old daughter was diagnosed with cancer, the entire campus was affected. Rather than withdraw, Dr. and Mrs. D. allowed us to walk beside them through their valley, crying and praying together. They showed us their love and trust in God in the midst of deep, dark pain. They invited us to sit at the bedside of a young girl who knew she would soon be with Jesus. They taught us to celebrate the good days, even baking her last birthday cake. They shared with us the harsh finality of death as we took turns standing watch by her casket for the wake. And amidst their tears, they shared our glorious hope in Christ as they led the entire student body in the song "It Is Well With My Soul."

The willingness of Dr. and Mrs. D. to reach out to hurting young people and to allow us to share in their darkest time made a profound impact on my life in ways that only God truly knows.

—Carolyn

5

THE HUNGER FOR IDENTITY

From the beginning,

life was unpredictable for Aaron. When he was six years old, his family emigrated from South Korea to the U.S., moving into a hope-depleting housing project near the trolley car turnaround at San Francisco's Fisherman's Wharf. In this hostile environment, every day was a fight for social "turf." So much for the Land of Opportunity.

Opportunity did eventually come knocking, though, in the form of a women's committee from a local Baptist church rapping on doors as they scoured the neighborhood for children to attend an upcoming program. Softened by their persistence, Aaron agreed to come. That's where he met Phil.

It didn't take long for Aaron to realize that his big-hearted, fun-loving Sunday school leader was willing to do just about anything for the young people of the church — including driving buses, organizing sports days and leading group hikes. When it came to seeking ways to befriend these toughened young people, nothing was too much for Phil; his childlike, boisterous love set the kids at ease.

As Aaron entered adolescence, he began questioning his life purpose. Who was he? What did God want of him? Why was he here? And how did the Christian faith matter in answering questions like these? Aaron approached Phil for guidance and found him willing to ask questions himself, to listen, and just to walk alongside.

While the neighborhood Aaron grew up in modeled violence and survival of the fittest, Phil modeled the lifestyle of the kingdom — by encouraging Aaron to discover his God-given identity. Through Phil's modeling, coaching and teaching, Aaron grasped how Christianity made sense. Aaron recalls:

> Phil understood my search for coherence and walked with me through it. He knew the scriptures well and was in deep relationship with God. Our conversations about the faith were not only intellectual and well-grounded, but fascinating and provocative. Phil demonstrated to me that following Jesus is not a theoretical exercise, unrelated to real life, but is a real and powerful way of living in a chaotic world.

The trajectory of Aaron's life was forever altered by the influence of this spiritually-anchored, fun-loving man who simply chose to invest in a wandering youngster from the projects. That was over 30 years ago. Today Aaron is an international business consultant and professor who is following in Phil's footsteps by mentoring young people.

Most people who hear this story think it was Phil's investment of time that yielded dividends in Aaron's life. What really happened,

"When I talk to young people
who are leaving the church,
the number one thing I hear is
that it's fake. It's fake. And kids,
young people can see right
through the façade. I don't blame
them. I wouldn't sign up for
something that is fake either."

–Pete Briscoe
Quoted From Grow Together Film

though, is more subtle. When we grasp this, we may find a whole new way to ignite hope for those hungering for a sense of who they are and why they are here.

The Peril of Purposelessness

All people hunger for an answer to the question "Who am I?" We desperately want to believe what Pulitzer Prize winning novelist Frederick Buechner says: "The place God calls you to is the place where your deep gladness and the world's deep hunger meet."[1] But we wonder: How do we get to this place? How can we can satisfy the world's hunger if we can't even satisfy our own?

It's a question of identity. Most people define their identities in terms of success: income, possessions and reputation. But at a deeper level, as bearers of the *Imago Dei*, we find ourselves tempted by two idols that poison our sense of direction. The first idol is *persona*. Today's online world makes it possible — easy, really — to transcend our circumstances and project an image of our hoped-for selves. Is this projection an illusion or reality? Do we even know, and would we admit it if we did?

Second, we are tempted by the idol of *tribe*, wrapping our identities around hobbies, musical taste, athletic ability or some other cultural preference we share with those we approve of or whose approval we hope to win. Ironically, we root ourselves in that which cannot last while uprooting that which can.

Through *persona* and *tribe* we come to believe that we are what we appear to be. But this train has only one destination: purposelessness. It's most acute among the young. As we saw earlier, only about one in five young people (ages 12 to 22) expresses a clear vision of where they want to go, what they want to accomplish in life, and why.[2] People who lack purpose are characterized by anxiety, disappointment, discouragement and despair.

And yet, age is no respecter of life purpose. When I ask audience members to "raise your hand if you've ever wrestled with the question 'What is God's will for my life?'" the only hands that don't go up are from people who didn't hear the question. The question of life purpose is a difficult one. And here is a little-known secret: Life purpose is not something we were ever intended to pursue on our own.

We Discover Life Purpose in Community

People *with* purpose are filled with joy, despite sacrifices they must make. They have a sense of energy, experience satisfaction when they accomplish their goals, and display persistence when they run into obstacles.[3] Older adults who have purpose live longer than those who don't.[4]

The most purposeful people are those who make it a point to be around happy, purposeful people. The Framingham study on heart disease — going on since 1948 — found that every contented person you know increases your likelihood of being contented by 2 percent. For every discontented person you know, your likelihood of being discontented rises 4 percent. In other words, unhappy people are twice as damaging to your state of mind as happy people are good for it.[5]

This kind of connection can happen at church, but only under certain conditions. One study of older adults found that meaning and purpose in life are significantly related to shared religious engagement.[6] If we just show up out of obligation and don't connect with others, church has little effect on our well-being. But people who show up, connect with others, and get involved as volunteers *live on average five years longer than those who don't.* So if you thought that the ornery kids in that Sunday school class were killing you, they're not — they're actually keeping you alive.

Lots of people regularly attend church, though, and don't find direction for their lives. Is there anything churches can do to help them find a source of energy and purpose in their work, in their family life, and in their community?

Yes. A recent study of young adults who stay involved in church revealed that they do so because of meaningful relationships in which they learn to live thoughtfully, make a meaningful contribution, succeed at work, and connect with Jesus in a real and meaningful way.[7] These are deep identity-shaping activities.

The church's influence in helping people discover and live out their God-given design goes far beyond caring, as important as that is. It is actually based on a theological truth unique to Christianity.

How Patterns of Purpose Emerge

For nearly 40 years, Arthur F. Miller has been offering a perspective on understanding design.[8] God has designed us with the motivation to achieve certain outcomes, Miller teaches, and we each feel drawn to fulfill those specific purposes as if pulled by a magnet.[9]

As people employ their God-given design, patterns emerge that Miller calls "motivated abilities." Miller shows that motivated abilities are of supernatural design, that they cannot be explained by cultural circumstances, that they cannot be added to or taken away from, and that they exist even in hardship and tragedy. According to Miller, every invention, discovery or creative act in all of human history goes back to the motivated abilities God has placed inside those inventors, discoverers and creators.[10]

So how do we discover these patterns in ourselves and others?

Connect to a Source of Purpose

We can only pour into others if we are being poured into ourselves. As Howard Hendricks famously said, "We lead out of the overflow of a quality life." My friend Julius Tajale demonstrated this in a workshop we conducted together in the Philippines. Julius held up a glass of water and asked, "Imagine that the water in this glass represents your potential for influencing others for Christ. How can you get the water to flow out of this glass?"

"By pouring it out," replied the audience.

Julius poured most of the water out and held up the nearly empty glass. The audience became hushed as it realized the implication: How many times had each of us been "poured out" and left feeling empty?

Then Julius took a pitcher and poured water into the glass until it overflowed. "Look, it is flowing out yet it remains full because there's a greater source of water pouring into it."

We need to be "poured into" so that we can remain full while overflowing into the lives of others. Here's an inventory of questions we can use to think about the inputs into our own lives:

- ▶ What does my relationship with God look like? How am I learning to know and love Christ more? What spiritual disciplines are a part of the fabric of my day-to-day life?
- ▶ Where do I see God at work in my life? In what ways do the people around me see God shaping me? How am I growing in my understanding of what it means to be redeemed?
- ▶ What kind of community do I have? What voices speak into my life and draw me deeper into my spiritual journey? What principles are my family, friends and work centered on?
- ▶ What is the big story I find myself believing? What about God's story do I find deeply compelling? How does this understanding shape my values and actions?
- ▶ Where do I find myself struggling? What pain points do I feel in my faith journey? In what ways are my beliefs about God, church, self and culture incongruent with how I act?

▸ What do I long for? What truly makes me tick? What do I daydream about? What captivates my imagination? What do I find myself thinking about every day?

Tell Our Story

Our identities are shaped in community through stories. Unfortunately, it is possible to know people for a lifetime and never really hear their stories or tell them ours. Change that. Start with, "We've known one another a long time, but I'm not sure we've really ever had a chance to share the stories of our lives. Can we take a bit of time to do that? I can go first if you like." Consider including:

▸ A little about your life history (your family, where you've lived, etc.),
▸ Some of your hobbies, likes and dislikes,
▸ What a perfect day looks like for you,
▸ Harder experiences in your life that have shaped you, and
▸ A snapshot of your hopes and dreams.

After sharing, you'll probably think of other questions that focus on identity. And that's healthy.

Ask Questions

Helping another person discover purpose and identity is a matter of cultivating, not manufacturing. You don't have to be a professional. Keith Anderson and Randy Reese explain:

God's heart has already felt and loved and hoped before we ever arrived. The songs of our soul have already been whispered and sung into our souls. *If this notion is true, and we believe passionately that it is, then the work of the mentor is not to create but to notice, not to invent but to discern.*[11]

The message is this: "God is working in both of our lives. I see what God is doing in your life, and I want to be part of the process of him shaping you into who he wants you to be."

Questions are the key. It's what Jesus did. Paul Stanley points out: "Jesus asked 288 questions in the gospels. He already knew the answers to all of these questions, but he asked them anyway. It just shows how important questions are in the relationship to spark thinking, involvement and responsibility."[12]

Deep questions aren't necessarily best. The best questions open up a process of discovery:

▸ Have you had experiences that thoroughly captured your imagination? What do you think was happening in those experiences?
▸ What are some experiences where you've accomplished something that gave you a tremendous sense of satisfaction? What do those experiences have in common?
▸ Tell me some stories, as detailed as you can remember, about things you've done that returned energy to you and made you feel more alive.
▸ What kinds of things do you like to work with (ideas, tools, etc.) and in what situations?

Be on the lookout for what the other person likes to *work with*, in what *situations*, with what relationship to *people*, and for what *outcomes*. There's no magic. Just understanding and awareness.

Share What We Know

A few years ago, my friend Joy told me the story of attending a Bible study with her mother, a longsuffering woman who had put up with a husband who despised her church involvement. Joy said:

I have always admired my mother's pluck. I don't think I could put up with what she does. I finally got to the point where I was mad at God. Hot tears rolling down my cheeks, I finally blurted out to a group of older women at church, "My mom has been following God all her life. Where's her reward? Why doesn't God bless *her*?"

This group of older women listened and then one said, "Did it ever occur to you that *you* are her blessing? Your marriage to a godly man, your devotion to the Lord's work, your children being raised in a happy home? If she could choose between an easier life for herself or a godly marriage and children for you, I'm sure she would choose it for you. *God hasn't forgotten her. You are her reward.*"

A simple act of community, a tender listening ear nested in a wise word from an experienced voice, and Joy's perspective completely changed. Indeed, she moved beyond bitterness to the true embodiment of her name, Joy.

Let God Tell His Story

In his autobiography *Creativity, Inc.*, president and co-founder of Pixar Studios, Ed Catmull, reveals the drama behind the emotionally complex movie *Up*. Even though it is an animated feature, viewers are drawn deeply into the story of the main character, Carl Frederickson, who copes with his wife's death by using helium balloons to turn their home into an airship and embarking on a South American adventure. Frederickson is accompanied by an insecure young scout, Russell, who is trapped on Frederickson's porch as the house is hoisted aloft.

Up profoundly explores themes of love, grief, significance, honor, caring and hope. But the story told in the film version looks nothing like the story as originally conceived, which featured a castle in the sky, two brothers quarreling over the throne, and a tall bird that helps them understand one another.

Only two elements of this original story survived: the title, *Up*, and the tall bird. If the original story had been carried through to the screen, it almost certainly would have been a failure. Few people are moved by castles in the sky and quarrels between privileged youngsters.

Sometimes our determination to tell a certain story with our lives blinds us to the textured, complex and soul-filling story God is telling. Will we clunk along in our own stories or let God tell his?

Satisfying the hunger for identity requires community, particularly personal, life-on-life relationships. This much is clear. But there is a deeper issue still. It's one thing to know that we have a stable identity that gives purpose to our lives. It's another thing altogether to know that our identity — our purpose — *matters* in the bigger scheme of things. This is the hunger for meaning, and I discovered it in a whole new way in an alcove of London's Westminster Abbey.

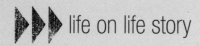 life on life story

BIG Brother

The mentor who has been the most helpful to me is Rosey Grier, humanitarian and NFL legend. As soon as I got my life straightened out and my priorities in line, the Lord gave me a BIG brother. Some friends told me I should meet with Rosey. We had a breakfast one morning, and we both knew immediately we were supposed to do something together. Initially we thought it would just be in San Diego, but in the more than 18 years since then our vision has expanded to the whole country.

I believe in seeking advice from people competent to give it. Once I identify someone I think can add to my life, I go after them. I did this with men a generation ahead of me like Rosey Grier, Ray Bentley, Bob Buford, Bob Kennedy, William Pollard and Ken Blanchard. Being aggressive is definitely a key to getting through to successful people. Perseverance is one of the things this caliber of mentor looks for when deciding if they want to spend time with you. They figure if a simple "no" will turn you away like a puppy, they're not going to waste time with you. You can't run with the big dogs if you stay on the porch.

—Estean

6
THE HUNGER FOR MEANING

London's Westminster

Abbey features dozens of gigantic monuments to persons whose historical achievements may have been modest but whose families possessed substantial-enough means to memorialize them in grand fashion. In their midst, one monument stands apart, small and unpretentious, as if to reflect the petite frame of its honoree rather than his gigantic, nation-shaping spirit. Tucked in a side alcove, the monument to William Wilberforce might go unnoticed but for a 21st-century revival of interest in his tireless opposition to the trans-Atlantic slave trade.

Invited by Abbey personnel for an after-hours visit, I stood before the Wilberforce monument, journaling my thoughts amidst the fading echoes of the day's last departing guests. Evensong approached, awakening the Abbey's mighty organ, its massive pipes curling the joyous sounds of heavenly anthems into every transept, calling forth living believers into eternal community with the saints entombed beneath the Abbey's stone floor.

At just that moment, my eyes fell on a phrase chiseled into the base of the Wilberforce monument: "He was among the foremost of those who fixed the character of their times." I felt a chill. My eyes stung, hot. This was a man fully alive. *Death comes*, I realized, as if for the first time. But then a vow: *God helping me, I will be fully alive as long as I have breath.*

Perhaps you've had a moment where you craved aliveness of the sort that enables you to shape, rather than be shaped by, the times. Our hearts long to know that our existence isn't incidental to what really matters.

For most, the search is solitary, and thus futile. Alone, our cries for meaning dissipate in the poisonous atmosphere of self-pity or echo back insufficiently sharp to penetrate the busyness of the day or the cacophony of the age. Our search for meaning needs something more than what we alone can bring to it. But what is it?

Years ago when I began work as a professor, I noticed the question of meaning on the lips of each of my students, no matter how gifted or talented or popular. It is a question that demands, but rarely receives, an answer, and it often sounds like this:

If I Were to Disappear, Would Anyone Notice?

Most of us can only look at Wilberforce's legacy with wistful envy. We hunger for truth, for identity, for meaning, but do not know how to find them. We scavenge the platitudes with which we were raised but find them self-defeating.

Layered over with strips of papier-mâché optimism and the watery glue of self-confidence, our outer forms become a way to hide the emptiness we feel inside. I recently encountered a website called *The Experience Project* in which people discussed questions such as, "Would anyone miss me if I disappeared?" My heart ached with pity as I read:

"I'm sure my parents and maybe my brothers would for a while, but I've left no lasting impression on anyone in my life."

"I just don't actually believe that anyone genuinely cares enough to miss me if I were to vanish. Of course my family would have the police looking for me because I was supposed to be somewhere or do something, but after a while, life would go on and no one would remember me."

"If I were to disappear, I believe that people would be relieved. I caused nothing but trouble for so many years and I think I am a burden."[1]

In other words, *I believe the real me — the deep part of me I know is not imaginary — has no actual value to anyone else.*

The hunger for meaning will be met, either by the good, the true and the beautiful, or by their counterfeits, by self-obsessions incapable of giving to others or receiving from God. Sometimes our quest for meaning is one of the things preventing us from finding it.

We Act on What We Believe

As the father of four teenage children, I've read through each *Lord of the Rings* book twice and watched each movie at least three times. My heart beats to Aragorn's speech on the eve of the battle for Gondor:

> Sons of Gondor! Of Rohan! My brothers! I see in your eyes the same fear that would take the heart of me! A day may come when the courage of men fails, when we forsake our friends and break all bonds of fellowship. But it is not this day. … This day we fight! By all that you hold dear on this good Earth, I bid you stand! Men of the West!

"The body of Christ is not
broken up by generations.
This generation should go
over here and do this thing
and that generation should go
over there and do that thing.
... If you saw the younger
and older generations come
together in a truly unified way,
you would see revival, you
would see change locally;
you would see change
nationally, globally. I don't
think there's anything
more profound that
can happen."
—Jon Bell

Quoted From Grow Together Film

I want to be in that army, part of a winner-takes-all battle against a snarling, ugly foe.

But when the speeches are made, the rush of inspiration they produce masks a debilitating lie: that the only path to meaning is a heroic stand against a singular evil. For most, this is not our lot. Ours is, rather, an intrepid life of thousands of little daily decisions, each inconsequential but together signaling what we truly believe about the meaning of life.

The epic-battle-myth obscures the fact that humanity's search for meaning is not as much a forward movement into the unknown as a battle against what we know all too well — the seemingly unconquerable meaning-killers that seep into our everyday existence. Meaning-killers such as:

Hopelessness: A sense of dejection, inadequacy and desperation pervades our nation. About one-third of high school students feel sad or hopeless.[2] Eighty percent of people polled say they believe it is harder to get ahead than it used to be.[3] And it's not just among youth. The highest levels of suicide in America are among white men over 85 years.[4] Hopelessness abounds when people feel powerless to make life better. Hopelessness is a parasite to meaning, destroying the very thing off which it feeds.

Consumerism: The average American sees as many as 5,000 advertising messages per day, from billboards to t-shirts to web pop-ups to television ads.[5] New breakthroughs even make it possible to identify a person's age, race and gender when walking through the mall and to instantly customize electronic billboards to feature ads similar people found compelling. Very soon advertisers will even be able to merge the virtual and real worlds, using social media profiles to recognize a shopper's face and offer special deals from nearby stores.[6] Through this targeting, we begin to identify ourselves primarily as consumers rather than producers. We exist only when others think we might buy something. No money, no meaning.

Habits: Sometimes our habits, embraced initially to ease hope-lessness, curve back and erode meaning, leaving us ever further from a source of hope. A study of Christian young men found that those who reported using pornography also reported lower levels of religious practice, lower self-worth, lower identity development regarding dating and higher levels of depression.[7] In a study of 20-somethings' faith, sociologist Jeremy Uecker found that although young people can (and do) return to faith from just about every circumstance, certain life habits such as co-habitation, extramarital sex, and drugs and alcohol accelerate diminished religiosity.[8] Sin leads to disordered love — loving the wrong things in the wrong way at the wrong time. Disordered love destroys meaning.

Ruptured relationships: "Shalom" is a Hebrew word describing peace with God, peace from war and peace with one's neighbors. To wish another person *shalom* is to wish that person completeness, safety, physical health and wellness, prosperity, tranquility, contentment, and friendship. God originally created human beings in a state of shalom — wholeness in their relationship with him, with each other, and with creation. In the fall, each of these relationships was ruptured. The world we see is not the way it's supposed to be.[9] Psychologist Mihaly Csikszentmihalyi studied the daily habits of Americans and gauged how much "flow," or sense of well-being, they experienced when doing various things. People reported the lowest level of flow when they were alone with their demanding "self." Even leisure did not necessarily improve the quality of life.[10] In fact, one of the most common leisure activities, watching television, was correlated with the lowest level of flow.

The way we live our lives can deaden a sense of meaning in life. But might it also enliven it? Yes, and in the most surprising way.

Too Earthly
Minded

In ancient Rome, Christians were often considered atheists because in becoming like Christ — the God-man who came to earth and experienced life as a human — they feasted joyfully together and focused on physical acts such as easing the suffering of the sick and poor. This earthy focus offended Roman sensibilities. Peter J. Leithart explains: "Instead of ascending past sensible things to the intellectual realm, Christians said that God had made Himself known in flesh and continues to give Himself in water and wine, bodies and bread. Christians were so earthly-minded that they could be no heavenly good."[11]

So earthly-minded that they could be no heavenly good. It's the opposite of the accusation lodged against Christians today. Such a thing is only possible in a world where the good, true and beautiful actually exist as a physical unveiling of spiritual wholeness rather than a spiritualized masking of physical imperfection.

We sense in our hearts that a world of goodness, truthfulness and beauty would, by definition, be a meaningful world. But what would it actually look like?

The Good: togetherness. In all the universe, the church is the natural home to what is robust, fruitful, victorious and full of ultimate meaning. Not just in *a* church, as in a particular church building, but in the universal church, the body of Christ, a group of losers for whom perfection is a far-off dream and who flail, toddler-like, steadied by God's ever-patient hand, until at last we grow up and become a beautiful bride. Not individually, mind you. *Together.*

Sociologist Peter Berger has noted that being together with other believers is one of the key factors that makes a serious faith plausible: "To have a conversion experience is nothing much. The real thing is to be able to keep taking it seriously; to retain a sense of its plausibility. This is where the religious community comes in."[12] The church serves as an "authoritative community" that gives people of all generations a sense of place, nurtures them, helps them grow spiritually, and teaches them to treat those inside and outside the community with dignity and love.

Recent studies have shown the power of "authoritative communities" in people's lives, helping children and adults live mentally, emotionally and spiritually healthy lives.[13] Churches ought to be the most purposeful authoritative communities. No church is perfect, but every church ought to be a safe place to practice the life of the kingdom rather than just a place to go on our day off.

The True: practical wisdom. In ancient times, Greeks saw wisdom as a spiritual state, other-worldly and detached. Plato (428-348 BC) saw wisdom as an unattainable form, about which we could know only enough to want and love it.[14] Lucretius (99 to 55 BC) taught that absorbing the teachings of the wise separated people from the striving masses so they could live a life free from pain, fear or struggle.[15]

In the Hebrew tradition, though, wisdom was not a state of restful repose. In Hebrew, the dominant word for wisdom is "*khokmah*," which means "skill in living."[16] While the Greeks saw wisdom in party clothes and looking a lot like *leisure*, the Hebrews saw wisdom in overalls and looking a lot like *work*.

From a biblical perspective, wisdom is truly multi-generational. Some young people are wise; some older people are not. As Job 32:9 says, "Great men are not always wise; neither do the aged understand judgment." Think of Solomon, proclaimed in scripture as the wisest of men. Solomon started off as wise but became more foolish the older he got.

Today scholars say that the optimal age for wisdom development is between adolescence and the mid-20s.[17] Wisdom is a virtue that must be cultivated, and it is best nurtured in youth. Preparing for a life of wisdom while you're young moves you toward what scholars call "gerotranscendence," *away* from superficial social engagement *toward* concern for others, meaningful relationships and contributing to society.[18]

We grow wise together, across the generations.[19]

The Beautiful: soulish embodiment. The Christian conception of humans is that we possess both natural, material bodies and supernatural, immaterial souls. Our souls rule our bodies, disciplining them in accordance with God's eternal law.

The reigning ideology of our age, on the other hand, is that humans are merely bodies — computers made of meat, as Marvin Minsky so hideously phrased it.[20] Based on a false understanding of the Apostle Paul's differentiation between the "spirit" and the "flesh," though, some Christians make the opposite mistake — exalting the soul and considering the body a sort of prison from which the soul longs to escape.

This teaching isn't new, and it doesn't come from the Bible. It's an ancient heresy called Gnosticism or Manicheism that taught that material existence was the cause of all evil and that humans can only be saved by a spiritual act of denouncing the body.

The biblical perspective is far different. Genesis 1:26 says, "Then God said, 'Let us make man in our image, after our likeness.'" The words "image" and "likeness" (shape and resemblance) are physical terms symbolizing authority over a certain domain.[21] God's domain is the entire universe, but rather than setting up a statue, God took the dust of earth, breathed into it, and created a living, moving representation of his image.

As image-bearers of God, we don't give shape to ourselves, nor do we resemble some abstract form. Instead, we take on God's "shape" and resemble *him* as sons and daughters resemble their parents. All human life is meaningful if for no other reason than that we bear God's image and experience the good, the true and the beautiful in real life.[22] But what does this sort of image-bearing look like in the church?

What Embodiment Looks Like

It took a near tragedy for Calvary Community Church in Westlake Village, California, to connect the generations in a way that satisfied the hunger for meaning. Drew Sams, pastor of student ministries, shares the story: "For years we had tried to make students 'busy for Jesus' by providing exciting events and programs that they would want to do." Drew's youth group was thriving, but everything came to a screeching halt when one of their top students — a young man who was involved in leadership, small group and missions — attempted suicide. Shocked, Drew and his team realized they had labeled this student a "success" while knowing nothing of his struggles.

That's when it hit them: No other spotlight in the world can illuminate the heart the way a personal relationship can. With that realization came a paradigm shift; what their youth ministry needed was to shift its focus from numbers, events and a full calendar of ministry activities to life-on-life involvement with their students.

Drew describes how this paradigm shift has played out: "One of the many practical ways we have [brought about this shift] is through equipping volunteers, parents and students to be present in each other's lives. Our events calendar is emptier than it used to be, but now we are free to go to students, listen and care unconditionally for them."[23]

This is a picture we ought to embrace all across the lifespan. Scripture describes the spiritual life as a birth and the church as everything from a family, to a team, to an army, to a flock. These metaphors have two things in common: We grow, and we grow *together*. No one can deliver a baby by email or nurse it by Skype or teach it to walk through texting.

The only way to show rising generations that church is something you *are*, not something to *go to*, is to make it *personal*. It's like a birthday party, not a drive-through. A wedding reception, not a concert. A family reunion, not an amusement park. But knowing this in theory does us little good. If what we've learned so far in this book is true, our own hunger for truth, identity and meaning will be satisfied only as we meet others' hunger. So how do we do that in a practical way?

 life on life story

A Life of Service

My aunt was a true servant for the Lord. She lived with us for five years when I was growing up, and her example had a profound impact on me. She modeled simplicity, showed hospitality, gave sacrificially and went out of her way to care for the needs of those around her.

One type of ministry that was particularly dear to her heart involved taking a group of severely mentally and physically handicapped adults camping for a week each summer. My aunt loved these trips and invited me along with her to help with their feeding and hygiene needs or to take them to the beach. She felt pure joy that God could use her to show love to others.

Her example and encouragement was so deep that I told my husband that one day I hoped we could adopt a child with special needs. Then, when we did just that, my aunt moved in with us at 71 years of age to help with our child's care. She was a true servant and truly changed the lives of dozens of people.

—Beth

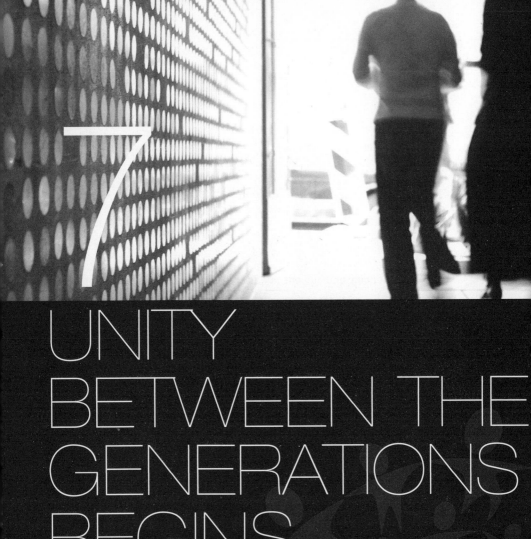

7

UNITY BETWEEN THE GENERATIONS BEGINS WITH YOU

We all hunger

for truth, identity and meaning. Our hunger is satisfied only in the context of multigenerational, personal relationships. Most people find themselves intimidated by the idea that they personally ought to form such relationships: *I have so little to give,* they say. But this betrays a manufacturing, not a cultivating, mindset. What we have to give is a matter of quality, not quantity. It's an issue of moments, not minutes.

My friend Crystal discovered this on October 8, 1978, through a simple yet life-changing comment from someone she hardly knew.

It was a mild day in Wichita, clouds covered the sky and the trees suggested a hint of fall foliage. Poring over the church's financial documents, Crystal absent-mindedly answered the ringing telephone only to hear her husband's physician say, "I'm sorry to inform you that Jack has cancer." The doctor continued, clinically but with compassion, "My colleagues and I think he has perhaps a year. I'm sorry we don't have a treatment that will make much of a difference, but you do have some time to prepare."

Crystal thanked the doctor and dropped the phone into its cradle. The world moved in slow motion, overtaken by a shadow of fear. At that moment, sprightly 80-year-old Robert Brewer stepped into the office. "Good morning ladies," he said pleasantly, looking every part the church treasurer in his dark tan suit and suspenders.

The secretary and Mr. Brewer exchanged a few whispered words, and Crystal saw him nod somberly. She knew they were talking about her and about Jack, and the reality suddenly struck her: *My husband is dying.* No amount of blinking could stop the tears.

Slowly, Mr. Brewer made his way to Crystal's desk. "May I sit down?" he asked, gently. Crystal nodded, dabbing traces of mascara off her swollen eyes.

For a moment, Mr. Brewer just sat. Crystal grabbed a tissue, apologized and reached for the checks she knew he had come to sign. But he stopped her with a gentle touch. "I want to share something with you, young lady," he said. *How odd of him to say that — I'm 54,* Crystal thought. Then she stiffened, bracing herself for the 'God-has-a-plan' recitation she was expecting. She was wrong.

"I always thought my wife and I had a good marriage," Mr. Brewer said, "but those last six months when she was dying of cancer, there was no comparison. Your faith will grow stronger. You will draw closer. It will be beautiful."

In the audible silence of the moment, Crystal heard God whisper through those words of wisdom from an elderly man who didn't hesitate to dive past surface superficiality to rescue a drowning soul.

An hour later, Crystal arrived in Jack's hospital room. He took her hand and Crystal's brave front failed. She laid her head down

"I think people have a sense of fear like, wow a mentor, what do I do? And it's really pretty simple. You just ask, what have I learned in life, what have I experienced, and how in the course of things I do can I naturally bring younger people along and impart that wisdom to them? It's really incredibly simple and natural when we start asking what can I impart to the next generation. Anybody can do it."

—Sean McDowell
Quoted From Grow Together Film

and sobbed as Jack stroked her hair. Neither said anything for the longest time.

Finally, Jack broke the silence. "It's going to be bad, you know. Maybe I can do something to shorten it."

Crystal's breath caught in her chest. "No, Jack, that's not the way." Then Mr. Brewer's words came floating back. *It will be beautiful.* "We're going to live life to the hilt," she said with a brave smile.

Jack gave her an odd look, and then grinned. For the next five months, they did live life to the hilt. Romantic dinners. Prayers together. Holding hands. A tiny puppy to be Crystal's companion after Jack was gone. Just before he died, Jack said, "I do not understand it. I am dying and I am so happy. There is *love* just oozing in every crack in this house."

To think that Jack and Crystal's last months together were redeemed by Mr. Brewer's four sentences. An investment of a *minute* became a *moment* that transformed suffering into love, and desperation into grace.

As we've seen, life-on-life relationships are the key to personal transformation. They've changed the church and the church, in turn, changed the world. It's the church's true secret. But what stops us from achieving this radical transformation is, more than anything, a simple failure to turn the minutes of life into moments of eternal significance.

Is it possible to tap the fuller potential of our relational moments in a way that satiates the world's hunger for truth, identity and meaning?

Minutes and Moments

"Israel discovers oil," blared the op-ed column in the *New York Times*. Through interviews with Israeli business people, the author Thomas Friedman had discovered that Israel's richness in ideas more than compensated for its lack of natural wealth. People with good ideas, Israeli geothermal expert Lucien Bronicki proclaimed, "are our oil wells."[1]

In terms of material resources, Israel is at an unquestionable disadvantage. But our world isn't just material. We have thoughts, hopes, dreams, strategies, interests, relationships, loves, passions, talents and drives. Whether we start with little or with much doesn't matter. One-talent people and one-talent nations are just as welcome and capable of stewardship as two-talent and five-talent ones.

In any given situation, there are two factors at play: actual and potential. The *actual* can be inventoried: time, money, land and so forth. Its supply is limited. There are no such limits to *potential*. The two different words for *time* used in the New Testament beautifully illustrate the difference between actual and potential:

Chronos: the quantitative passing of time; minutes.
Kairos: the qualitative value of time; moments.

Chronos refers to the passing of time. We can measure it. In fact, measuring it is the whole point. Chronos is the word from which we get our words chronicle, chronology and chronograph, which are ways of recording events in the order they happened, whether historical events or fractions of a second. It's a central concept in a manufacturing world.

Kairos, on the other hand, refers to the *potential* of time. It cannot be measured; it is always "now." Make the most of every *kairos*, the Apostle Paul wrote (Ephesians 5:16). In God's economy, temporal *minutes* are valuable because they are potential eternal *moments*.

It was Mr. Brewer's stewardship of a couple of actual minutes with Crystal that turned their encounter into a cultivating moment full of potential and great significance.

"You can be mentoring quite a bit watching a baseball game with your son rather than sitting him down and saying, 'Now I want to tell you three things this morning.' You know he doesn't want it that way. Incidental-to-life mentoring takes place much more effectively because truth is taken without intimidation."

–Ravi Zacharias
Quoted From Grow Together Film

God is the master of transforming minutes into moments. In his upside-down kingdom, the passage of time pales in significance compared to the last becoming first, the hateful becoming loving, the poor becoming rich, the powerless becoming mighty and the broken becoming whole.

Given the chronos and the kairos, the belief that *I have little to offer* is actually an affront to God. It assumes that God is limited by the resources we think exist, and it treats with contempt the value God brings to bear in his very-good world, teeming with life.

Relational Moments

My friend Juergen Kneifel's father died when Juergen was only 10 years old. Caring men in his church reached out to Juergen. They didn't counsel him or even pretend to. They just took him to ballgames and included him on family camping trips. Their example of being fathers to the fatherless (James 1:27) motivated Juergen to begin Mission2Mentor and has made him a respected leader in the community of people who advocate youth mentoring.[2]

The call for mentors is threatening to many people, though. Few people will sign up for relationships when they have to deal with problems they don't know anything about. One mentoring ministry representative I spoke to said she had 600,000 young people she had not yet been able to match with mentors. It's just too uncomfortable and too scary.

But I'm convinced that the unwillingness to invest in at-risk people of any age is rooted in a radical misunderstanding of what relationships are all about. For some of us, life is an assembly line — there's no fun to it, just duty. For others, it's all about comfort — hang around people who make us feel good and ignore everyone else. For still others, it just seems overwhelming to think of having people unload their problems on us and not know what to do, so it is best to just lay low and leave it to the experts.

Speaking personally, the only time I break through this mindset is when I realize that:

God is not asking me to give what I do not possess. God does not expect me to be a licensed psychologist or seminary-trained theologian. While I want to continue to learn and grow, what I know now is enough for now.

It's OK to start slow and grow. No one starts running by participating in a marathon. In a relational sense, God is guiding me through every stage of training, starting with small investments in others — a short note, a quick phone call, a Facebook message, a hug — and working my way up to cheering at their ballgames or throwing some extra potatoes in the pot and hosting a meal. Little investments invariably lead to bigger ones, such as in-depth talks about life.

My mess is my message. The real art to relationship is to be honest, not to impress. It's hard enough to form relationships across generations without being invited to a perfect meal at a perfect house for a perfect conversation. Forget perfect. Be real.

It's OK to admit that I don't know. Just because God places me in a situation doesn't mean I know what to do. Saying, "I don't know what to do. Can we pray about it?" is just as valid, maybe even more so, than saying, "Oh, I've been there. Here are your action steps."

As a perfectly-contented introvert, I found that the more I shared in these small ways, the more I was able to open up and become genuinely vulnerable with others, and that "not having any technique" is what brought untold blessing into my life through multigenerational relationships.

How Much of My Life Should I Share?

I was a new professor at Bryan College and had just spoken for the first time in chapel. A student shuffled into my office and asked, "Will you mentor me?" In my mind, I formed a picture of him dangling a set of handcuffs, ready to fasten himself to me for life. I told him, "No." Of course, he left my office disappointed. I wish I could replay that scene from my life, knowing what I know now.

Part of my problem was that as a young professor, I didn't know how to appropriately relate to students outside of class. I didn't want to be their buddy, but I didn't like the idea of being a boss either. Relationships across generations can be tricky like that. If you disclose too little, the other person may see you as being cold and distant. But if you disclose too much, the other person may feel uncomfortable.

Sociologists Irwin Altman and Dalmas Taylor studied interpersonal disclosure and explained that the best relationships "scaffold" the level of self-disclosure. As you take the lead by being a little vulnerable, others will usually reciprocate. When they do, you can disclose a little more.[3] This builds a foundation of trust and raises both individuals' comfort levels.

In order to arrive at the right level of openness and vulnerability, reflect on these questions:

- ▶ Is this level of sharing appropriate for this stage of the relationship?
- ▶ Does the way I am sharing my past glorify sin?
- ▶ What are my motives for sharing this information in this way?
- ▶ Am I burdening others with information they shouldn't have to shoulder?

In many cases, sharing our wounds with others is a healthy part of the healing process. My friend Joe Couch explains it this way: "Wounds fester and carry disease and, if untreated, can easily infect others nearby. When a wound is dealt with properly, however, it becomes a scar. Scars leave a mark on your life and tell a story, but they are no longer dangerous."[4]

Recently, and with some trepidation, I shared with my children some of the devious things I did when I was a kid. My fear was that it would give them bad ideas or enable them to justify wrong actions. It could lead to sin. But I realized that invulnerability can be a sin, too. It's the sin of pride — and pride does not become less sinful just because I think others will be better off if I am prideful.

At the end of the discussion with my children, my then-10-year-old son said, "Papa, I am glad to know that you were a bad boy. I had no idea you struggled with the things I struggle with." What followed was a conversation with deep vulnerability, drawing us closer together.

How Past Sins Affect Future Relationships

Many people have told me, "It is best if I don't try to influence younger generations because of the things in my past." We need to expose this thinking for what it is: self-righteousness. True righteousness does not mean having no record of wrongdoing — it means having our record wiped clean by Jesus. The Apostle Paul declared,

> Do you not know that the unrighteous will not inherit the kingdom of God? Do not be deceived: Neither the sexually immoral, nor idolaters, nor adulterers, nor men who practice homosexuality, nor thieves, nor the greedy, nor drunkards, nor revilers, nor swindlers will inherit the kingdom of God. And such were some of you. But you were washed, you were sanctified, you were justified in the name of the Lord Jesus Christ and by the Spirit of our God (1 Corinthians 6:9-11).

As author Susan Hunt explains: "God is the Redeemer of those failures. Those failures are part of God's story in you."[5] Consider how you can appropriately share your struggles and failures and explain how God is working in your life: *It's embarrassing to admit my sins. I've made many tragic errors that have hurt a lot of people and dishonored God. Because of my past I must rely completely on God's grace and his offer of forgiveness.*

There are two ways in which past sin ought to affect future relationships, though. First, it should affect the kinds of relationships that are appropriate to form. If you've struggled with alcohol, you ought not to have meetings over a glass of wine. If you've struggled with pornography, you ought not to meet one-on-one with people like those who were of sexual interest to you. If you've struggled with being domineering or bossy, maybe you should make it your goal to ask questions or give encouragement rather than to take leadership.

Second, past sin should affect future relationships in the way you tell your stories. If you used to struggle with anger, but God has enabled you to experience joy, make that part of your story and tell it. If you've been healed of some sort of substance abuse or undisciplined behavior, make that part of your story and tell it. If you've been convicted that your feelings of superiority were actually arrogant hypocrisy, make that part of your story and tell it. Tell the story — without dismissiveness, justification or glorification.

Start Now

God's message is clear: It is through relationships in the context of the body of Christ that people's hunger for truth, for identity and for meaning are satiated. People are hungry, and you are the one with the groceries. Let joy replace fear and start cooking. *It will be beautiful.*

You don't need to be a professional. In fact, that could get in the way. In 2003, Watermark Community Church in Dallas was a small group of believers meeting in a warehouse. One of those believers, Bill Roberson, joined with another like-minded man to start a small group Bible study. "Most of these people had never had any life-on-life discipleship in their Christian walk," Bill recalls. "Most of us were just dropped at the church doorstep to figure it out on our own." Soon there were 400 people in these groups being discipled by 60 leaders, and Watermark itself had grown to upward of 5,000 congregants. The church doesn't staff this effort. There is no budget. And yet so many congregants are involved in this grass-roots movement that life-on-life discipleship has become the norm church-wide.[6]

God doesn't ask us to steward resources we don't possess, but he does ask us to get our priorities straight. Lynn Harold Houg says, "The tragedy of the world is that men have given first-class loyalty to second-class causes, and these causes have betrayed them."[7] One second-class cause by which I find myself constantly betrayed — and you may as well — is the belief that *getting along* is at odds with, and more important than, speaking truth. Is it possible to be friendly with someone and also help them grow?

 life on life story

Speaking the Truth in Love

Relationships create the opportunity to speak the truth in love to those we mentor. More important, it allows them to listen without feeling judged.

Earl and his wife Linda went out of their way to show me they cared about me and what was happening in my life. They provided the spiritual guidance that was missing in my home, and in many ways they were like a second set of parents for me (they even taught me how to drive). I knew they cared about me and wanted the best for me.

Case in point: One day, Earl saw me out in the community behaving in an unchristian way. As soon as I saw him, I knew he was disappointed. Later, when we talked about it, he gently explained that I had been working so hard to be a Christian example and then I had allowed people to see me in a way that did not bring glory to God.

Someone needed to say those tough words to me, but I think only Earl could have said them with such grace that I would be able to hear them and recognize the truth in them. And the great thing about it was that after that hard conversation, Earl never brought it up again.

—Dan

8

SPEAKING TRUTH WHEN OTHERS DON'T WANT TO HEAR IT

The levees

were everything. If they did not hold, hundreds of people would be dead by morning. Cor van der Hooft, mayor of the village of Willemstad, knew the fierce storm combined with the spring tide threatened his village, and that it was his job, in spite of the late hour, to warn people to flee for safety.

But there had been similar threats before and nothing had happened. Was this a false alarm? It was hard enough being mayor without having everyone irritated at him for waking them in the middle of the night with a message of doom.

Van der Hooft paced back and forth. Suddenly the door opened with a crash, rain spilling in along with a breathless member of the warning party: "Mayor! They aren't listening to us!"

Life and death in his hands, Van der Hooft's face transformed into an expression of fierce determination. He shouted, "The people's lives are in mortal danger. You must wake them whatever the cost. Break windows. Yell and scream. They have to know you are serious."

That frigid night, the North Sea overwhelmed the Netherlands' levees in 400 places. Thousands lost their lives. But in the village of Willemstad, with its "alarmist" mayor, only two people perished.

Cor van der Hooft's dilemma wasn't whether or not to act. All wise public officials know it is better to be safe than sorry. But leaders the world over also recognize that telling people what they don't want to hear is a risk — you could be wrong and lose credibility.

Fortunately for the people of Willemstad, Van der Hooft overcame his trepidation and saved hundreds of lives. Many leaders fail to act with similar resolve, not because they don't know *what* to do, but because they are afraid of how they will be perceived if they do it. It's difficult to speak forthrightly to people who don't understand. This reticence is a serious problem when it comes to reuniting the generations in the church: How difficult and risky it can be to communicate truthfully across generations.

The Risk of Speaking Truthfully

Telling people what they need to hear is hard. Both older and younger generations struggle with it, saying things like, "Other generations' 'truth' is so different," or "Other generations don't want to hear what I have to say."

This is not a question of the content of truth claims. It is a question of *truthfulness* — whether what we say is fully true. In the gospels, Jesus didn't avoid conflict. In fact, he intentionally hung

"The right truth must be taught, but you can have all the right truth in the world, you can be absolutely orthodox in your beliefs, but if it's not lived out in relationships it will never change your family, it will never change the church, and it will never change the world."

–Josh McDowell
Quoted From Grow Together Film

out with his critics, having meals in the homes of Pharisees and those who knew their lifestyle was wrong. Jesus spoke truthfully — sometimes as an encouragement, sometimes as a warning. But his propositional truth statements were always couched in demonstrated concern for those hearing his message. Most commonly, Jesus communicated truthfully through relationship, engaging his audiences with questions and often turning away from eager crowds to focus on his small group of disciples.

It makes no sense to embrace Jesus' *message* while abandoning his *method* of delivering it. And there are at least seven aspects of speaking truthfully, without which it is difficult for our hearers to relate in a way that advances truth in their lives.

Truth Can't Be Heard Without ...

Maturity

Buddies and bosses. Many in the older generation think they have to choose one or the other. They don't want to come across as bossy, so they choose to be buddies. The buddy's highest goal is to be *with* someone. The relationship itself is the point. Of course, being a buddy is not in itself a bad thing. God made us for relationship with him and with each other.

But hanging out doing things like eating pizza and playing video games, while fun, risks making the problem worse. Today, the National Academy of Sciences has redefined adolescence as the period extending from the onset of puberty, around 12, to age 30.[1] Chap Clark states what ought to be obvious, that the greatest need of adolescents is for "adults to become adults."[2] When adults won't grow up, they lose a sense of meaning, and so do those who count on them for guidance.

It's good to be a buddy, but it's not enough. Each person we reach out to is plagued by sin, pain, immaturity, weaknesses and blind spots. Jesus was absolutely *with* his disciples. He was literally walking along the road with his disciples for 13 months out of his three years of ministry.[3] That's a lot of hanging out. But Jesus also confronted the disciples when necessary and prompted deep growth. This was possible because of ...

Friendship

Sociologist Christian Smith defines love as self-expenditure for the genuine good of others.[4] Love is the basis for true friendship. In his best-selling book *The Friendship Factor*, Alan Loy McGinnis says that "friendship is the springboard to every other love."[5] Shortly before his death, Jesus told his disciples, "No longer do I call you servants ... but I have called you friends."[6]

Friends don't just hang out. They love each other enough to listen, to challenge, to care for and to confront. All of these are important. Yet according to a recent study, the number of Americans who said they had no relationships like this has tripled since 1985.[7] Friendliness may be common, but friendship is rare.

Friendship is demonstrated through more than words. Psychologist Albert Mehrabian found that 93 percent of our communication is through posture, facial expressions and tone of voice, while only 7 percent is through words.[8] If you want to be taken seriously, you have to be a friend. But that's not all. You can be a friend and still not be credible if you don't have ...

Experience

Experience is more than just bringing your collected wisdom to bear on a relationship. It involves moving alongside others to relate your life to theirs. We each have hopes, dreams, victories, disappointments, passions, gifts and struggles. What is God teaching us together through these?

"Anybody who does
say I feel qualified to
be a mentor, I'd be very
concerned about right
from the beginning. You
have to have humility ...
the one thing you don't
want in a teacher
is pride."

–Ravi Zacharias
Quoted From Grow Together Film

If what we've seen already in this book is actually true, we can't really grow unless we have these kinds of experiences together across generations. "Come, follow me," Jesus said. What he was going to show them was so remarkable that they could not have discovered it on their own. For three years, they saw him eat, cry, sleep, get angry, show compassion, debate, discuss and love. And this experience went both ways. Who did Jesus want to be with on the eve of his death? His friends.[9] They were so close that at the Lord's Supper, the apostle John reports actually leaning against Jesus. Imagine two friends today giving each other a big hug or putting their arms around one another's shoulders.

Social scientists have studied these sort of tight-knit relationships and concluded that "strong bonds depend on the ability to understand and respond empathetically to others' experiences."[10] The key word here is empathy; not having pity on another person (that's *sympathy*) but seeing things the way the other person sees them. Yet experiencing life together isn't complete just through caring. It also involves …

Exploration

Most mature Christians will say that their spiritual growth has involved honest wrestling with significant issues. When we fail to give people space to wrestle in a similar fashion, we're basically saying to them: "We've already done your thinking for you — here's the correct prepackaged conclusion." Such an approach is especially noxious to younger generations. My friend Ken Van Meter conducted dissertation research with top Christian school students and found that if students believed that Christianity was being forced upon them, they became resistant to the biblical worldview message.[11]

Importantly, the resistance is not to the message itself but to the way it is presented. Bill Perry, founder of the Recon generational college ministry model, explains: "The established generation is more interested in the bottom line (truth, biblical worldview, right answers, etc.) and in getting there as quickly as possible. Not so with the emerging generation. For them, it's as much about the journey as the destination."[12]

In Luke 10:26, a hostile lawyer asked Jesus a question about eternal life. Instead of giving an answer, Jesus replied, "What is in the law? How do you read it?" In the culture of that time, asking questions was a way of sharing truth. It's a tradition worth recovering, and the most mature Christians I know seem to do it naturally. They aren't threatened by wrong answers. Rather, they catechize by discerning — not dictating, and by inviting — not inventing. Do we trust God enough to surrender the outcome to him rather than manipulating our way to it? Exploration is critical, but it must be done in a spirit of ...

Connectedness

In many churches, it is assumed that teaching occurs when a pastor preaches or a Sunday school teacher gives a lecture. This isn't the main way Jesus taught, though. He occasionally addressed the crowds, but mostly he walked and talked, discussed, asked and answered questions, told stories, engaged in debates, and used outdoor activities to get his point across.

It is said that a good teacher is like a candle, consuming itself to light the way for others. Teacher and author Parker Palmer says that all good teachers give of themselves to connect in this way: "Good teachers weave a fabric of connectedness ... and the loom on which they do the weaving is their own heart."[13]

As our friend, Pastor J.R. Kerr, points out: "The established generation asked, 'Can you prove it to me?' The emerging generation asks, 'Can you *hear* me?'"[14] Listening is especially crucial for young adults who live amidst cultural pluralism and need to know that we understand the tensions that causes. It isn't just connectedness with students, though, or even with whatever subject they are wrestling with. It's connecting rising generations to a lifestyle of ...

Practice

In a recent Summit Ministries' course, one of our lecturers gave a compelling talk about the value of traditional marriage up against the same-sex marriage movement. He invited questions, the first of which was: "OK, so the weekend before I came here my uncle was at my house sharing how excited he was to marry his same-sex partner. Help me understand how I should relate to him if what you're saying is true." For the rising generation, the discussion of deep moral and philosophical issues does not take place in a vacuum. Young Christians are unlikely to embrace a biblical doctrine they can't imagine presenting credibly to their non-believing friends and relatives.

Practicing is essential to *learning*. The director of General Electric's education program, which has a multibillion-dollar budget, put it this way, "I wish I could tell you that courses are the key, but they are not. When we ask our people to write down the outstanding development experience of their lives, only about 10 percent cite formal training."[15] If this executive is right, 90 percent of learning is in practice, not in lecturing. Jesus called his disciples so they could be *with him* but also so that he might prepare them to preach and to have authority over the spiritual world.[16] Jesus' methods have been rigorously studied, and today overwhelming evidence suggests that practicing, mentoring and coaching are the best ways for people to learn and grow.[17]

Truthful people have to be willing to say, "Let's look into that together." Truth is hard, but it becomes much more manageable when we have company on the path leading to it. But accompaniment is usually unwelcome unless it is accompanied by ...

Sincerity

Flattery gets you nowhere in multigenerational relationships. One of our Summit students confided in me, "People are always saying my generation is awesome, that we will save the world, but they're putting a lot of pressure on us to do things we don't think we can do."

Saying things like, "You're so smart," or "You're so talented" can backfire. Research conducted by Carol Dweck and her colleagues demonstrates that praising people for their *intelligence* causes them to care more about performance and take fewer risks (because their failure might disappoint others). People praised for their *effort*, on the other hand, displayed fewer low-ability attributions ("I'm not capable of doing this") and greater task persistence, enjoyment and task performance.[18]

Everyone needs encouragement, but truly helpful encouragement focuses on effort and character — what those you're influencing have done and how you saw it. Saying, "You are such a kind person," isn't as helpful as saying, "You were being compassionate when you sat with the new kid at youth group last week." Similarly, saying, "You're tough; you can do this," isn't as helpful as a more specific comment such as, "I've seen you keep your commitments time and again, and I know you're capable of doing what you've set your mind to."

Sincerity acknowledges that we are all flawed people. It doesn't seek shortcuts. Instead, it acknowledges that we will make mistakes and expresses confidence that by walking together we can persevere.

To summarize, just being a *knower* of the truth doesn't make a person a *lover* of the truth. Loving the truth means loving people and learning how to communicate truth without being bossy.

Speaking Tough Truth Without Being Bossy

As we saw earlier, the two extremes in multigenerational relationships are being buddies and being bosses. Most relationships are more nuanced than either extreme, but how do you know if you're tending toward one or the other?

If you form relationships without any sense of helping the other person grow, you're probably defaulting to the buddy mentality. When you form relationships as a means to an end, such as getting them to join the church or make some sort of spiritual commitment, though, you may be defaulting to a boss mentality of trying to fix other people and manage their growth.

If your goal is to journey with people and not think about the destination, you're probably defaulting to the buddy mentality. On the other hand, when you focus on controlling the outcome of assenting to truth rather than the journey of arriving at it, you may be defaulting to the boss mentality.

Often churches in pursuit of efficiency and measurable growth try to hype members into joining accountability groups to acknowledge sin, Bible reading programs to enhance Bible literacy or growth groups that focus on improving outward behavior. Unfortunately, as good as these outcomes are, they can miss what God is really after — not well-behaved moralists but people who love him with all of their hearts, souls and minds.

At the end of the day, though, I must admit that I sometimes doubt whether it is actually possible to rise above my personal goals to speak truth in love. Such doubts are put to rest by an experience I had as a college student. As a rising senior at my university, I was elected student government president. I quickly realized I didn't have very good leadership skills or the stomach for the in-fighting and chaos that are often part of student politics.

Fortunately, a mentor came to the rescue, though in a totally unexpected way. Her name was Mary Rowland, and she was our university's executive in charge of student life. The first thing I remember Dr. Rowland saying to me was, "This could be the best year of your life or the worst year of your life, depending on whether or not you listen to me."

As you might expect, I recognized the bossiness of this statement and instinctively began to reject it. But as Dr. Rowland helped me put together a successful strategic planning retreat, make peace between various student groups and turn that year of student government into a great success, I realized she was committed to walking with me and helping me become the leader I had the potential to be. Sadly, Dr. Rowland died just one year later. Her influence remains, though. I have yet to pass an entire day without drawing on the lessons she taught me.

It's OK to be direct and have strong opinions, but that kind of relational style only works when underlying it is a trust built on truthfulness, safety and sincerity. How to form those sorts of relationships, where steady growth takes place and community togetherness thrives, is what we will focus on next.

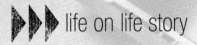 life on life story

That's What Friends Are For

I was involved in full-time ministry for 25 years before returning to the marketplace. As a young pastor and teacher, I eagerly sought out older, more experienced mentors. Some were educators or church leaders, but many were businessmen or craftsmen who served as elders or volunteers.

These older men taught by example and I learned by emulating them. Sometimes the roles were formalized, as when I served under a board, but usually the relationships were informal: We participated in the same accountability group or worked at camp together. Thanks to their modeling, I became a better husband, father, neighbor, teacher and follower.

I still look to older men as mentors, only now they are my peers. A group of us — all in our 50s and 60s — meet regularly at a restaurant for what we call "Life on Tap." We come from different backgrounds, professions and churches, yet we share a common faith and a committed friendship. We listen, learn, stimulate and encourage one another. We talk candidly about everything. No subject is off limits. No question is too far out. We don't always agree, but we don't judge.

Most of us are mentoring younger men in our families, at our jobs or in a ministry context. Our time together helps recharge us for these relationships.

—Mike

9

A SAFE WAY TO DEVELOP NEXT-GENERATION LEADERS

Late 1970s.

I was still in grade school when my family moved from Detroit to a small town in Kansas. Our tiny new church offered no youth programming, so during the Wednesday evening prayer meeting, my brother Scott and I played outside. It was a recipe for trouble. One night we tried to make a bomb out of Dixie cups, masking tape and gasoline. Of course it spilled and we set the parking lot on fire. No people or cars were harmed, fortunately.

The next week, oddly, a prayer meeting for boys had started. The leader, Don, got down on his knees to pray and encouraged us to do the same. We knelt there in awe, eyes screwed shut, mostly, as Don spoke to God with simplicity and reverence.

Recently, just months before he died from cancer, I visited Don. He and his wife Angel sat with me at the dining room table to chat and cry.

We all knew it would be Don's and my last visit this side of eternity. Toward the end of our conversation, we prayed together. As I prepared to leave, Angel said, "I want to show you something." We walked over to the fireplace where she pointed out a small grease stain on the brick hearth. "When this fireplace was brand new, you and Scottie cooked hotdogs and some grease dripped here. Every time we see the stain, we pray for you guys."

For 35 years this couple had prayed for my brother and me every time they came near their fireplace. Clearly, the bond between us wasn't just about prayer meetings or making sure the youth were gainfully occupied on Wednesday nights. In their minds, my brother and I and the other young people who had passed through their doors had never really left.

Our presence in their home was renewed every time they lifted us up to the Heavenly Father by praying over a grease stain. Don and Angel were formative in my brother's and my leadership development. Both Scott and I are in full-time ministry today, and without a doubt our line of influence runs through their family. They walked with us in order to send us ahead in a stronger, straighter way.

Though we've focused in this book on how to keep people from walking away from the church, it's not really about butts in seats. True cultivation results in *fruitfulness*, fruitfulness produces seeds, and seeds, properly stewarded, produce harvest after harvest. In human terms, it's called leader development. It doesn't happen automatically, even in the presence of strong leadership. Leading people is one thing; turning them into leaders is another.

As our conversation about uniting the generations draws to a close, let's look at practical ways cultivating relationships not only keeps rising generations from walking away, but actually prepares them to carry out the work of the ministry and similarly equip those who come after them.

Safe With the Shepherd: The Environment of Leader Development

In addition to metaphors about cultivation and growth, the metaphor of "shepherd" in scripture reveals a uniquely biblical kind of leadership. The word occurs more than 100 times and aptly describes the kind of leader who creates a safe place for people to satisfy their hunger for truth, identity and meaning.

Shepherds are leaders who appear to be following those they lead. As Harvard professor Linda Hill explained after learning about Xhosa shepherds in South Africa, "A leader is like a shepherd. He stays behind the flock, letting the most nimble go out ahead, whereupon the others follow, not realizing all along that they are being directed from behind."[1]

This is God's way. Psalm 23 talks about God as a shepherd who is both with the sheep and guiding them. In his book *Mentoring for Mission*, Gunter Krallmann calls this let's-walk-together approach "transparent with-ness."[2] Transparent with-ness transcends idiocy (*idios* is the Greek word for what we alone know) and blossoms in *koinonia*, or knowing community.

Through transparent with-ness, shepherds put their charges at ease so they can more easily take risks. Safety is to leadership growth what a net is to a trapeze artist. People are freer to grow when their learning is cushioned from the consequences of catastrophic failure.

People who feel unsafe, though, leave. As long as they have the power to choose, people will avoid places where they feel bullied or left out or manipulated. There's nothing gut-wrenching about it. Abandoning an emotionally unsafe place is as easy as avoiding a tiresome song by switching to a new station.

"I think that God's 'Plan A' for mentorship and cross-generational ministry happens in the family. I think God wants parents to teach and to train their children in the way they should go. And there should be a natural mentorship and relationship in that."

–Esther Fleece
Quoted From Grow Together Film

Here's an uncomfortable fact: The young adults leaving the church are not leaving other places. They're not leaving their parents. An unprecedented number of them are still living at home. They're not leaving their friends, either. Rather, they're running away from places where they don't feel safe. Like church.

So if we don't want the rising generation to run away, we have to create a safe place for them to grow. But how is this done? Aren't *safety* and *growth* incompatible goals? Is it possible to string up a safety net without having people use it as a hammock? Keep in mind that *safe* and *comfortable* are not synonyms. Our goal is to create the kind of space in which we intentionally encourage those walking with us to take risks, to leave behind excuses and rise to their full potential so they can positively influence every area of society. The best way to keep people from running away, it seems, is to send them out.

To mentoring guru Paul Stanley, challenging people in a climate of safety is all in how you ask it. When Paul needs to confront someone he's developing as a leader, he usually begins with an observation: "I've observed a couple of things. Could I have your permission to just shoot straight with you?" Then, crucially, Paul seeks to *expand* the issue rather than *narrow* it. For example, Paul says things like, "Tell me a little about that. How do you see it? Have you ever seen it before? What seems to prompt it?"

Asking questions gets people to think about how they might change their own behavior. This kind of confrontation doesn't protect people from growth; it frees them to achieve it. And it does so for a reason that has been known for many years by persuasion researchers.

People Persuade Themselves

A man convinced against his will is of the same opinion still. It's an old saying, but none the less true for its age. When people feel free to choose, they're less defensive. Good questions awaken people to truth: "How are you acting on what you know to be true? How are you not?" or "How do you think God intends for you to handle this situation?" or "Where is this decision going to take you and is that where you want to go?"

Questions tap into humans' deep need to arrive at conclusions for themselves. When others persuade us, we're always aware of having been persuaded. When we persuade ourselves, our convictions seem to be more authentic. They're deeper. They last longer.[3]

In addition to question-asking, gentleness is an important tool of self-persuasion, as was demonstrated in one odd but memorable piece of psychological research. Researchers put children into a roomful of toys, discerned which toy each child was most interested in, then forbade playing with that toy using either a severe threat ("You may not play with that toy anymore or you'll be in big trouble.") or a mild threat ("You shouldn't play with that toy. It's not good."). Children given the mild threat were significantly more likely to avoid the forbidden toy, even when brought back nine weeks later. The mild threat gave room for children to persuade themselves to avoid the forbidden toy of their own volition.[4] In other words, gently-worded commands had longer-term positive consequences than strongly-worded ones, at least with children.

Jesus' yoke, his body of teachings, was clear-cut, but it was also gentle (Matthew 11:29). Gentleness doesn't back away from the truth; it walks *with* truth and invites others to do the same. For instance, my friend Rick grew up without a father and was intimidated by tough, stern men like the worship pastor of his church, Pastor Richie. But when Rick experienced a bout of chronic depression, Pastor Richie reached out with gentleness, helping Rick sense God holding him in the palm of his hand. Fourteen years later, my friend still thinks of Pastor Richie as a life-long model of Christian manhood.

For some, gentleness sounds like an encouraging word from a person they expected to criticize them. My friend Mike once took his three children on a steam locomotive ride through Connecticut's Naugatuck Valley. Noticing an elderly gentleman watching his children squabble, Mike half expected a lecture about parenting. Instead, the man said, "It's OK. Keep it up. You're doing a good job." Those 10 words, spoken in five seconds, encouraged Mike for years.

For others, gentleness sounds like an assurance of love. My friend Marci once told me about being confronted by a mentor for stubbornly refusing to admit a lie. Her mentor told her, "I will love you no matter what, and even if you're not ready to confess, I'm still going to love you."

Harshness says, "You did this, it was wrong, and you're bad." Gentleness says, "You could do this great thing — rise up!"[5]

The idea that walking alongside people is the best way to help them is perhaps more familiar in the workplace than in the church. In the workplace, it's called "coaching."

Coaching in the Church

The word "coach" often refers to an athletic instructor, a mentor or even a New Age guru teaching people to channel their inner power. At the root, though, a coach is one who leads another by walking alongside and helping that person maintain forward motion. Coaching is a serious component of most business training programs for two reasons: First, it allows newer employees to practice with a safety net. Second, it allows those in charge to guide newer employees in a more relational way.

Coaches call forth capacity; they're less concerned with the quality of any given decision than they are with their protégés becoming great decision-makers over the long haul.[6] Coaches create *space* for people to grow and encourage them to *act* on what they know and to take *responsibility* for their actions. In one study of executive coaching, trainees who were coached for two months after a training event out-performed by 400 percent those who attended the event but were not similarly coached.[7]

Coach-trainer Tony Stoltzfus, among many others, has expanded coaching from the workplace to the church. He's found that regardless of the area of life, people perform better when others *believe* in them and express confidence that God is working in them, that they can solve their own problems, and that their coach is on their side.[8]

Coaches do three things differently from most conversation partners. First, they listen actively. Their focus isn't just on *hearing* what others say, but on making sure those people *feel heard.* Second, good coaches ask open-ended and broad questions and give others time to think. "Tell me more about that" become their five conversation-altering words. Third, coaches help others set worthy goals. They aren't satisfied when a conversation ends without at least some sense of direction. Their focus is on, "Where will you go from here, and how will you know when you get there?"

For me, it helps to have prepared questions to guide a coaching conversation. First, I ask *goal* questions like, "Describe where you would like to be." Then I ask *reality* questions like, "Where are you currently?" Then I ask about *options*: "What steps could you take to turn your thoughts into actions?" Finally, I ask *will* questions: "What are you willing to do, and how will you know when you've done it?" *Goal, Reality, Options* and *Will* form the acrostic G.R.O.W., which is easy to remember.

Lots of people are learning to use questions to help others break through life's logjams, and that's good. More and more churches have found these same techniques useful in achieving their goals of winning people to Jesus and helping them grow.

Churches can use coaching to create a safe way for people to relate across generations. At Hill Country Bible Church Northwest in Austin, Texas, church leaders have embraced coaching to the point of taking their leadership through coach training workshops. According to Annette Boorman, generations team leader at Hill Country, church leaders now use coaching questions to help people set goals for spiritual growth. Annette explains: "Our philosophy of ministry comes out in the three questions we ask: 'Who are you?' 'Where are you spiritually?' and 'How can I help you take your next step?'"

Before these questions will be taken seriously, Hill Country members have to know and genuinely care about people. That's where coaching comes in. Hill Country equips its congregation with basic coaching skills so they can connect with others across generations on a more meaningful level.

Recognizing that parents often have a difficult time conversing with their own children, Annette's team also uses coach training to help parents talk with their kids. Even if they begin with goofy questions like, "If you could only eat one thing for the rest of your life, what would it be and why?" Annette says it begins a dialogue that is the foundation for spiritual growth. Hill Country also sets aside time in their children's Sunday school classes for parents to come into the classroom to coach their own children.[9]

Coaching techniques can give people confidence that they are capable of influencing others across generations. And this brings us back to a question threaded throughout this work, how to specifically influence the Millennial generation, the generation rising into adulthood right now.

Influencing the Rising Generation

It's hard to teach an old dog new tricks, the saying goes. It isn't so much a rap against old dogs as it is a reminder to teach dogs what they need to know while they are young. It's true with people, too.

Ecclesiastes 12:1 says, "Remember also your Creator in the days of your youth, before the evil days come." Spirituality in youth has been shown by research to correlate to wisdom in *later* adulthood.[10]

Some people in older generations find it difficult to relate to people who are much younger. Perhaps they would find it easier if they understood how much the rising generation *wants* to be influenced by what's older. Take music, for example. In one survey, 81 percent of respondents between 16 and 29 said they liked the Beatles, whereas only 39 percent of respondents liked one of the most popular rock bands of recent times, Coldplay.[11] "Retro" is hip.

But whether it is hard for us to form relationships across generations is beside the point. It isn't *about* us at all — it's about God and his agenda. When we get on board with God, great things happen. For instance, my friend Blair, a principal at a Christian school near Seattle, invited five male students to join together to read Proverbs aloud and talk about how to act on it. Blair wrote to me, stunned at the impact of this simple gesture:

> We just came back from a spiritual retreat for our high school. These five boys took seats in the front row, without being asked, and stood and worshiped in front of the entire student body. At the end of the first day, I did a male-only session asking: "Where are the godly young men?" These young men stood and gave testimonies from the year about what God was doing in their lives and expressed their vision for the school. After they shared, other young men started to come to the microphone and share, dream, confess sins, ask for help and offer to help. It was amazing; young men who had never shared publicly stood and participated.

As we went through the second day of our retreat, students were not only caught up in worship, but they remained at the altar in tears and prayer even after being released for lunch. By the last session, the students surrounded the teaching staff, laid hands on them and prayed for them. The teachers were overwhelmed and stood in shock with tears running down their faces. Our speaker and worship band left on Tuesday afternoon, but the Spirit of God remains and has changed our school.

Proverbs 27:17 says that we should sharpen one another as "iron sharpens iron." Blacksmiths prepare swords for battle by lovingly and skillfully and repeatedly hammering them with a hard object. Blair wasn't the hard object. Scripture was. But by lending his presence as an older man, he turned a small group for boys into a sword of truth with which to do battle against spiritual apathy. That's catechesis in action.

No matter their generation, when people are approached from the standpoint of understanding, they usually respond with a strong desire to form relationships. Even the toughest young person longs to connect with a caring adult.[12] Multigenerational relationships not only help satisfy people's craving for truth, identity and meaning, they also, as we will see in the next chapter, strengthen the church to rise to the occasion when opportunities —or even terrifying events — arise.

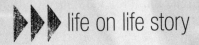 life on life story

Never Too Old

Marilyn Jarrett's nimble fingers deftly work a needle, bringing cloth to life in colorful threads as she carefully follows an intricate pattern. Embroidery is a passion of Marilyn's, but she has an even greater passion for seeing God's faithful hand reproducing the image of His Son in the lives of others through discipleship.

Retired schoolteacher Marilyn, 82, and a growing number of men and women at Zionsville Presbyterian Church in the Indianapolis suburb, see one-to-one mentoring as a gift, not a task. Marilyn has been mentoring Jill Tanner, a 48-year-old mother in her church, for about a year and a half.

Every two weeks, Jill drives down a country road to spend an hour or more at Marilyn's house. Beyond reading the materials together, their conversation inevitably moves toward events in Jill's life. Marilyn listens intently to Jill. Her guidance is both gentle and firm, blending the voices of friend and mother.

Since 1998, Marilyn has been intentional in her time with one or two women at a time, and she knows they too will be able to mentor other women, as several of them have already begun doing. Marilyn lives out 2 Timothy 2:2, entrusting the things she's learned to reliable women who will teach others.

Marilyn speaks from experience: "Anybody who wants to mentor can mentor. We all have something we can pass on to someone else." And as Marilyn has found, being a mentor is as much of a blessing to her as it is to the women she mentors. "I get as much out of it as they do," she admits. It is a gift she refuses to pass up.

[Excerpted from the article by Hayley Newsom on Cru.org, http://www.cru.org/training-and-growth/mentoring/to-learn-twice-marilyn-jarrett.htm]

10
RISING FROM THE ASHES

Our family station

wagon chugged up the narrow streets of Manitou Springs, Colorado, a quaint historical town aptly dubbed a Hippie Mayberry. At the top of a hill, there appeared an antique hotel painted yellow with brown trim. "This must be the place," my father said. I stared out the rear seat window at the sight. At age 17 and just graduated from high school, this was the moment of transition. From the two-week program I was attending in this place I would go straight to debate camp and then off to college, all in a matter of one month.

We walked inside the dimly lit lobby and came face to face with a tanned, athletic-looking man with huge glasses who introduced himself as Dave Noebel. All I knew was that his program, Summit Ministries, was supposed to help me find answers to my questions about God, the world and my relationship to both.

"I hear you have a lot of answers, which is good because I have a lot of questions," I said abruptly. It was rude, but Noebel wasn't threatened. He chuckled and said, "Fair enough. But first, I have a question for you. What do you have that is so worth living for that you'd be willing to die for it?"

The question startled me. *What do I live for?* Across the pages of my mind flashed images of people I knew who weren't really living as much as they were staving off death. Instantly I knew that I would live for something, that I would step across the line to move my generation.

My Summit experience changed everything. Not all at once, but like the burst of a thruster that ever-so-slightly alters a satellite's trajectory, it moved me gently into a new orbit of purpose, conviction and courage.

*****

Fast forward 29 years. I had, at the invitation of Dave Noebel, become Summit's new president upon his retirement. But just six months into my tenure, I found myself sitting alone in my darkened office in full-blown panic mode. It was 1:30 in the morning. Through the window, I could see flames from the deadly Waldo Canyon wildfire licking their way over the nearby ridge, threatening to drop down into Williams Canyon and destroy our beloved little town.

The evacuation call had come at 1 a.m. Over the following days, the fire became the worst natural disaster in 30 years for the Colorado Springs area, consuming tens of thousands of acres of woodland and burning 346 homes to the ground. The following summer, another fire did even more damage. But my concern at that moment was more immediate: the lives and safety of 180 students, 40 summer staff, and around 30 full-time staff and their families.

When it was clear that our team was prepared for a safe evacuation, my thoughts turned to the heritage of our ministry. *What do you take when every trace of half a century of ministry could be gone by morning?* With the help of our staff, I piled things into my hatchback. Hard drives of pictures, documents and databases. Special artifacts. Decades' worth of board-meeting minutes. With moments to spare, I raced to catch the caravan of buses, vans and cars transporting 300 Summit students and staffers — including 27 children under the age of eight — to a shelter 15 miles away.

*****

Twelve hours earlier, I had been at a day-long workshop across town. Just after lunch, I stepped outside for some fresh air and looked up at the mountains. My heart nearly stopped. A column of smoke, visibly growing in intensity, rose from the direction of our town. I called our executive director, Eric Smith. "Where's the fire?" I asked.

"It's in Waldo Canyon."

This was really bad news. I've hiked and mountain-biked every inch of that canyon. There's no road access, no way to arrest a fire's growth.

"What is our evacuation plan?" I asked tentatively, recognizing how absurd it was for a ministry president to pose such a question.

Eric named a local church but then said, "They've already taken in another group — they can't help us."

"What is plan B?"

Eric mentioned a local Christian school but then said, "It's Saturday. We haven't reached anyone there yet."

"Let me check into a plan C and I'll get back to you," I said.

It was a wild card, but I had just had lunch with pastor Steve of Mountain Springs Church on the east side of Colorado Springs. "We need to find a way to introduce Summit to our congregation," Steve had remarked. I was about to test the full sincerity of his comment.

"Steve," I said when we connected, hoping the joking tone of my voice was clear, "I thought of a way to introduce Summit to your congregation."

"Great! What is it?"

"Well, we're going to need to evacuate because of the fire."

"No worries. We have plenty of space in our home and your family is welcome to stay here as long as you like."

"OK. But what if I bring 300 of my closest friends?"

"Oh, Summit. That's right. Well, let me check with our security guy at the church and we'll let you know."

A few minutes later my phone rang. "This is Rob. I'm the security guy at Mountain Springs. We heard Summit might have to evacuate?"

"Yes, you heard right."

"Awesome!" he enthused. *"We want you here."*

Tears filled my eyes. It's one thing to be taken in during an emergency. It's another thing altogether to be wanted.

"Let me know when you're coming and we'll be ready for you," said Rob.

Around 2:00 a.m., I caught up with the Summit caravan. Pulling into the parking lot, we were welcomed by the senior pastor, Steve, the security guy, Rob, and some hardy volunteers. They had, in fact, collected enough sleeping bags for half our group. We gave them to all the young women in the program and they trudged sleepily off to their building.

I turned to Steve. "We're going to need a lot of things — sleeping bags, food … all that."

"Don't worry," he said, just as enthusiastic as Rob had been the previous afternoon. "We sent out a notice on our Twitter feed. We'll get all the supplies we need."

I looked at my watch. Two-thirty in the morning. *Who on earth is checking their Twitter feed at 2:30 in the morning?*

Apparently, a lot of people. Within minutes a parade of head-lights appeared, coming down the access road. One by one they dropped off sleeping bags and cases of bottled water. One guy came directly from Walmart where he had purchased 10 cases of water and every sleeping bag in the store — probably $3,000 worth — without even knowing who needed them.

In the morning, students and staff woke to a piping hot breakfast provided by Golden Corral, Starbucks, Einstein Bagel Company and Costco (no, the Costco breakfast wasn't served one bite at a time on toothpicks, in case you're wondering).

In the first morning service, pastor Steve said, "Look, folks, we are going to need help with Summit. Imagine taking 300 people on a picnic for a week. What supplies would you need? Now go get them!"

And they did. Piles and piles of supplies: food, toothpaste, sham-poo, pillows, towels. The Mountain Springs community took the picnic comment seriously. They brought so many paper plates I think our stockpile will last halfway through the millennial reign of Christ. Those who couldn't bring supplies brought money. Exceed-ing, abundant provision.

During the second service, members of the congregation laid hands on our wide-eyed students and prayed for them, much to the surprise and delight of some of those who had not grown up in an expressive church tradition.

That night, we had one of the most powerful worship services I've ever experienced. After 24 hours of uncertainty and upheaval, a few hundred students, staffers and guests gathered to worship God in song. Despite the raging wildfire to the west, we knew through the love of the Mountain Springs community that God was in charge.

To talk to the evacuated students and staff, you'd almost think the evacuation was a fun field trip rather than a natural disaster. They proudly called themselves 3-Vac (Session Three Evacuees) and referred to their "Toasty '12" experience. T-shirts were made, of course.

In the space of six days, an eternal bond formed between the Mountain Springs and Summit communities. Blessed by the generosity of these adults they had never met before and would probably never see again, our students gave back by pulling weeds, dusting and refreshing the landscaping.

When we left campus the following Friday, one of the church secretaries started crying and said, "We don't want you to leave. Your students are our guardian angels." That night, after a specially-prepared banquet and graduation ceremony, one of our students confided in me, "When I came to Summit, I was an atheist. After being with these caring people — people who don't even know us — there is no way I can be an atheist anymore."

What's more, this was happening all across Colorado Springs. More than 32,000 people were evacuated. Churches stepped up and helped them. For one week, there were no denominations. And no generations. Young and old worked side by side, called together by an urgent cause.

If the church can respond this way in the face of a threatening wildfire, could it do so in a culture beset by evil and injustice? If the church can help an entire city find comfort in the midst of uncertainty, could it be a winsome advocate for truth in the arena of ideas?

*****

For Summit Ministries, the blessings continued flowing. One of our donors bought two sturdy diesel buses to replace two usable but aging vehicles that just wouldn't do in an evacuation. Little did we know that this one donation would save 52 lives.

Almost a year after the fire, one of our sturdy new buses was taking a group of students on a whitewater rafting trip when an impaired driver veered out of his lane and hit the bus head-on with his pickup. The pickup driver was killed instantly, but miraculously only our driver and eight students were injured, and all were released from treatment within a few hours.

It turns out that the new bus had saved them. Its weight and low center of gravity kept it from tipping over a guardrail and down a 30-foot ravine.

I tried to maintain my composure through multiple media interviews, but inside I was seething. How *dare* this pickup driver get behind the wheel impaired? Dozens of our students and staff could have lost their lives. In my heart, I wanted justice. But then a conversation with the mother of the dead man and an extraordinary meeting with the students who had been there changed everything.

Just before dinner that evening, I had gathered the students and staff who had been on the bus to let them process and pray. One after another, students thanked those who had helped them in that moment of crisis. Soon we were fairly exhausted with emotion.

"Do you have any questions for me?" I asked.

"What happened to the driver who hit us?" one student asked, gently.

I told them the man had died. There was an audible gasp. Death was not yet an ever-present reality for many of them.

"What do you know about him?" another asked. I told the students about my call with the driver's mother, who, in broken English, had begged my forgiveness and shared about her son, in his early 40s, and the tragic life he and his siblings had led. Three of her four children had already died.

The sound of sniffles filled the room. Time crawled. Then a student asked in a shaky voice, "Was he driving impaired?"

This was the question I dreaded most. *God help me*, I prayed, then said, "We don't know for certain, but from what the authorities say, it appears he was."

A long silence followed as students considered that they had nearly been killed by someone who should never have been behind the wheel. Then one young man rose and said, haltingly, "We didn't get to go rafting today because of the crash. I still have my refund. I want to give it to help pay the family's funeral expenses."

One by one other students rose and made the same declaration. By this time, most of us were weeping openly. Compassion and forgiveness had instantly replaced indignation. These young adults couldn't excuse the deed, but they could forgive the person, and they did.

The next week, our executives attended the funeral of the driver and delivered a check for $2,100 collected by our students, along with condolence notes. A week later, the driver's mother sent me a letter. "We have never been so loved in all of our lives," she said. On behalf of the students who had taught me forgiveness, I cherish that letter.

Many people have said that our attitude would have been different if any of our students had been seriously injured or killed. This is undoubtedly true. But during those moments visiting with our students, the best and brightest of their generation who in a few weeks would be headed to America's top colleges and universities, I was struck by the compassion of their response. They were eager to see this man's tragic life in the light of a creator who had knit him together in his mother's womb and knew all of his days before any one of them was lived.[1]

The experiences of the fire and the bus crash ultimately filled me with hope. So much is at stake for our nation and the world. The tragic consequences of sin have never been so much on display as during our lifetime. So few people understand the times and can discern the course forward.[2]

But I am filled with hope because of the church; the one place in all the world where people of every tribe and tongue, and of all generations, can proclaim God's message — that his son has set creation free from corruption and bondage and brought freedom and glory.[3]

Decades hence, people will look back at our age, with all of its potential, and ask whether we stewarded it well. May God unite us for his purposes, in his name, *across all generations*, for a time of revival and reformation the likes of which the world has never seen.

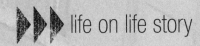 life on life story

Mentored by the Best

Businessman and social entrepreneur Bob Buford has had a profound impact on the church and marketplace through his co-founding of the Leadership Network and his popularizing of the concept of "Halftime." Bob was mentored by one of the giants of modern management, Peter Drucker, which enriched Bob's life and ministry. As documented in an article for *Time* magazine by Rick Wartzman:

(Their relationship) started with a letter that Buford wrote to Drucker, seeking his counsel on how to improve the performance of a business that was already growing fast. The next thing Buford knew, he was on his way to Drucker's modest ranch house in Claremont, Calif., for a one-on-one meeting. Things blossomed quickly from there.

"In terms of friendship, we were an unlikely pairing," Buford writes. "A generation apart in age. One of us spoke English with a heavy Austrian accent. The other spoke Texan. I owned a cable television company. Peter didn't even own a television. ... I followed the Dallas Cowboys. He followed Japanese art."

Yet for all of these differences, the two clicked. Their sensibilities and worldview were totally in sync. "In Peter," Buford explains, "I found a soul mate."

—Rick

ENDNOTES

Chapter 2

1 Readers interested in the history of evangelicalism might enjoy reading Joel Carpenter, *Revive Us Again* (Oxford University Press, 1997); Marvin Olasky, *Monkey Business* (Nashville, TN: Broadman & Holman Publishers, 2005); Richard Mouw, *The Smell of Sawdust* (Grand Rapids, MI: Zondervan Publishing House, 2000); and James Davidson Hunter, *Evangelicalism* (Chicago & London: University of Chicago Press, 1987).

2 Joel Carpenter, *Revive Us Again: The Reawakening of American Fundamentalism* (New York: Oxford, 1997), 139.

3 http://www.csmonitor.com/Commentary/Opinion/2009/0310/p09s01-coop.html

4 Win Arn, *The Pastor's Manual For Effective Ministry* (Monrovia, CA: Church Growth, 1988), 41

5 http://www.edstetzer.com/

6 George Barna, "Twentysomethings struggle to find their place in Christian churches," http://www.barna.org/barna-update/article/5-barna-update/127-twenty-somethings-struggle-to-find-their-place-in-christian-churches

7 William Damon, *Path to Purpose: How Young People Find Their Calling in Life* (New York: Free Press, 2009), 8.

8 John Mayer, "Why, Georgia?" from *Room for Squares*, Columbia Records, 2001.

9 Denis Diderot, *Rameau's Nephew and Other Works*. Garden City, New York (1956), 308.

10 Church historian Jerry Sittser said, "In the history of Christianity, knowledge has never been considered a virtue. Wisdom is a virtue, not knowledge." http://cross-map.christianpost.com/devotionals/true-knowledge-4195

11 Mortimer Adler, ed. "Chapter 101: Wisdom," *The Great Ideas: A Syntopicon of Great Books of the Western World* (Chicago: Benton, 1971).

12 Denis Diderot, "Diderot, Denis (1713-1784)," in Ronald Hamowy (ed.), *The Encyclopedia of Libertarianism* (Thousand Oaks, CA: Sage, 2008), p. 125.

13 "Manufacture," in http://dictionary.reference.com/browse/manufacture

Chapter 3

1 Pitirim Sorokin, *The Crisis of Our Age* (New York: E.P. Dutton, 1941), p. 326.

2 See Philip Jenkins, *The Next Christendom* (New York: Oxford University Press, 2011).

3 Will Durant, *The Story of Our Civilization, Part I, Our Oriental Heritage* (New York: Simon and Schuster, 1954), p. 1.

4 Will Durant, *Story of Civilization, Vol. VI: The Reformation* (New York: Simon and Schuster, 1980), p. 190.

5 Christopher Dawson, *Religion and the Rise of Western Culture* (New York: Image Books, Bantam Doubleday, 1957), p. 24.

6 Luc Ferry, *A Brief History of Thought* (New York: Harper Perennial, 2011), p. 60.

7 For more information, see the December 2012 *Summit Journal* at http://www.summit.org/media/journal/2011-12-Summit-Journal.pdf.

8. The idea that humans are slaves of the gods was ubiquitous in ancient Near East cultures, according to Kenneth J. Turner ("Teaching Genesis 1 at a Christian College," unpublished paper). This is particularly true of Islam. The Qur'an consistently refers to people as slaves of Allah. See, just as a starting point, Suras 2:23, 2:90, 2:186, 2:207, 3:15, 3:20, 3:30, 3:61, 3:79, 3:182, 4:172, 6:18, 6:88, 7:128, 7:194, 8:51, 9:104, 10:107, 14:11 and 15:49. The Arabic word is "abd" which means one who is totally subordinated. Badru Kateregga says, "The Christian witness, that man is created in the 'image and likeness of God,' is not the same as the Muslim witness." See Badru D. Kateregga and David W. Shenk, *Islam and Christianity: A Muslim and a Christian in Dialogue*, electronically available on The World of Islam: Resources for Understanding CD-ROM published by Global Mapping International, 5350.

9. Walter Kaiser, *Toward an Old Testament Theology* (Grand Rapids, MI: Zondervan Academie, 1978), p. 100.

10 Ibid., pp. 106-107.

11 D.A. Carson, *The God Who Is There: Finding Your Place in God's Story* (Grand Rapids, MI: Baker Books, 2010), p. 20.

12 The title may be just two words, but the subtitle of Rutherford's book runs to 136 words, making clear that it was an argument against the monarchy: "Or the Law and the Prince; A dispute for The Just Prerogative of King and People: containing the reasons and causes of the most necessary defensive wars of the Kingdom of Scotland, and of their Expedition for the aid and help of their dear brethren of England; in which their innocency is asserted, and a full answer is given to a seditious pamphlet, entitled, 'SACRO-SANCTA REGUM MAJESTAS,' or The Sacred and Royal Prerogative of Christian Kings; under the name of J.A., but penned by John Maxwell, the excommunicate Popish Prelate; with a scriptural confutation of the ruinous grounds of W. Barclay, H. Grotius, H. Arnisæus, Ant. de Domi. popish Bishop of Spilato, and of other late anti-magitratical royalists, as the author of Ossorianum, Dr. Ferne, E. Symmons, the Doctors of Aberdeen, etc. In Forty-four Questions.

13 In his first treatise, John Locke argued that all of us — not just kings — are heirs of our first father, Adam. For a full text, see http://www.lonang.com/exlibris/locke/

14 See Alvin J. Schmidt, *How Christianity Changed the World* (Grand Rapids, MI: Zondervan, 2004).

15 Rodney Stark, *For the Glory of God* (Princeton, NJ: Princeton University Press, 2003), p. 291. The entirety of Stark's chap. 4, "God's Justice: The Sin of Slavery," should be carefully studied by all Christians.

16 See C.N. Jeffords, "Sin," In D.N. Freedman, A.C. Myers & A.B. Beck (Eds.), *Eerdmans Dictionary of the Bible* (Grand Rapids, MI: W.B. Eerdmans), p. 1124. See also See Joel F. Wiliiams, "Way," In D.N. Freedman, A.C. Myers & A.B. Beck (Eds.), *Eerdmans Dictionary of the Bible* (Grand Rapids, MI: W.B. Eerdmans), pp. 1370–1371. Williams says, "In the concrete sense, a road (Deut. 1:2; Ruth 1:7) or a movement along a particular path, i.e., a journey (Exod. 13:21; 1 Kgs. 19:4). However, Heb. derek was also employed more broadly. To walk in the ways of God meant to live according to his will and commandments (Deut. 10:12–13; 1 Kgs. 3:14). In Isaiah, "the way of the Lord" can refer to God's provision of deliverance from enslavement or exile (Isa. 40:3; 43:16–19). The word was often used to identify the overall direction of a person's life, whether righteous or wicked (Judg. 2:17–19; Ps. 1:6; cf. Matt. 7:13–14), wise or foolish (Prov. 4:11; 12:15). In the NT, Gk. hodós has a similar range of meanings. In Mark's Gospel, it is used repeatedly to present Jesus as "on the way," i.e., on his journey to Jerusalem (Mark 8:27; 9:33–34; 10:32). The broader context adds a deeper significance to these more literal references, since Jesus' willingness to go the way of suffering provides an example for his followers who must also prepare to suffer (Mark 8:31–34). In John 14:6 Jesus claims to be "the way," i.e., the only means of access to God (cf. Heb. 9:8; 10:19–20). In Acts, "the Way" functions as a title for the Christian message (Acts 19:9, 23; 22:4; 24:22) or the Christian community (9:2; 24:14)."

17 George Barna, "Most Twenty-somethings Put Christianity on the Shelf Following Spiritually Active Teen Years," http://www.barna.org/teens-next-gen-articles/147-most-twentysomethings-put-christianity-on-the-shelf-following-spiritually-active-teen-years

18. See "Divorce Rates and Church Attendance" at http://www.divorce.com/article/divorce-rates-church-attendance

Chapter 4

1 *The Epistle of Mathetes to Diognetus*, translated by James Donaldson and Alexander Roberts, http://www.earlychristianwritings.com/text/diognetus-roberts.html

2 Josh McDowell and Sean McDowell, *The Unshakable Truth* (Eugene, OR: Harvest House, 2011), p. 32. Reference is to Alan Hirsch of Forge Mission Training Network.

3 See, for instance, Romans 12:2, Colossians 2:8-10.

4 George Barna, "Only Half of Protestant Pastors Have a Biblical Worldview," http://www.barna.org/barna-update/article/5-barna-update/133-only-half-of-protestant-pastors-have-a-biblical-worldview

5 Sean McDowell. Telephone Interview. 15 September 2009.

6 John Stonestreet. Telephone Interview. 21 October 2009.

7 Seventy-five percent of people who leave church do so because they do not feel a sense of belonging. David D. Durey, "Assimilating New People Into the Church," 2000. From a doctoral dissertation, "*Attracting and Assimilating the Unchurched in the 21st Century.*" Found at garyrohrmayer.typepad.com.

8 I learned at the Yad Vashem holocaust museum in Jerusalem that the majority of Hitler's brutal SS officers had masters and doctoral degrees; education has its place, but it can make evil people more dangerous just as easily as it can make good people more virtuous.

9 Pierre de Chardin, *The Phenomenon of Man,* http://en.wikiquote.org/wiki/Pierre_Teilhard_de_Chardin

10 Today's U.S. economy is 30 times as big as it was 200 years ago (this is what economist Cleon Skousen calls the "five thousand year leap." Prosperity is spreading, which is having all kinds of effects, both good and bad. On the good side, an entire generation around the world is being rapidly lifted out of poverty. According to Scott Todd, extreme poverty has dropped in half just in the last generation, from 52 percent of the world's population to 26 percent. Scott Todd, *Fast Living: How the Church Will End Extreme Poverty* (Colorado Springs, CO: Compassion International, 2011), p. 37.

11 Lynne C. Lancaster, *When Generations Collide: How to Solve the Generational Puzzle at Work.* A presentation for *The Management Forum Series,* March 17, 2004. Synopsis by Rod Cox.

12 George Barna, "Young Adults and Liberals Struggle With Morality," http://www.barna.org/teens-next-gen-articles/25-young-adults-and-liberals-struggle-with-morality

13 Maggie Jackson's book *Distracted* is a must read. She asks: "Are we heading into a dark age? To ask this question is first to wonder whether we at present have much of a collective appetite for wrestling meaningfully with uncertainties, and whether we have the will to carve out havens of deep thinking amid the tempests of time." Maggie Jackson, *Distracted: The Erosion of Attention and the Coming Dark Age* (Amherst, NY: Prometheus, 2008), p. 213–14.

14 David Kinnaman and Gabe Lyons, *UnChristian: What a New Generation Really Thinks About Christianity … and Why It Matters* (Grand Rapids, MI: Baker Books, 2007), p. 45.

15 *Daily Mail*, December 18, 2006. http://www.dailymail.co.uk/news/article-423273/ Being-celebrity-best-thing-world-say-children.html

16 Christian Smith with Melinda Lundquist Denton, *Soul Searching: The Religious and Spiritual Lives of American Teenagers* (New York, NY: Oxford University Press, 2005). p. 118.

17 John Stonestreet. Telephone Interview. 21 October 2009.

18 Chap Clark, *Hurt: Inside the World of Today's Teenagers* (Ada, MI: Baker Book House, 2005), p. 53.

19 Kenda Creasy Dean, *Almost Christian: What the Faith of Our Teenagers Is Telling the American Church* (New York, NY: Oxford University Press, 2010), p. 30.

20 Raymond D. Aumack, "The Story of St. Patrick," http://www.iaci-usa.org/pdf/3-11%20enews%20stpatrick.pdf

21 "Solomon Stoddard," Wikipedia, http://en.wikipedia.org/wiki/Solomon_Stoddard

22 "Bethel Indian Town: David Brainerd's Early Work," http://gnadenhutten.tripod.com/ bethelindiantown/id9.html

23 Arnold Dallimore, *Spurgeon: A New Biography* (Carlisle, PA: Banner of Truth Trust, 2000).

Chapter 5

1 Frederick *Buechner, Wishful Thinking*: A Theological ABC (New York: Harper and Row, 1973), p. 95.

2 William Damon, *The Path to Purpose* (New York: Free Press, 2008), p. 8.

3 Ibid., throughout text.

4 Monika Ardelt, Effects of Religion and Purpose in Life on Elders' Subjective Well Being, *Journal of Religious Gerontology,* Vol. 14, No. 4, 2003.

5 http://articles.latimes.com/2010/jul/08/news/la-heb-sadness-happiness-infectious-diseases-20100708

6 Ardelt, Effects of Religion

7 https://www.barna.org/barna-update/millennials/635-5-reasons-millennials-stay-connected-to-church#.U5ImXPldWSo

8 Many of Miller's observations have been highlighted by Max Lucado in *Cure for the Common Life* (Nashville: Thomas Nelson, 2008).

9 Arthur F. Miller, *Designed for Life: Hard-Wired, Empowered, Purposed — The Birthright of Every Human Being* (Charlotte, NC: Life(n) Media, 2006), p. 42.

10 Ibid., p. 45.

11 Emphasis mine. Keith Anderson and Randy Reese, *Spiritual Mentoring: A Guide for Seeking and Giving Direction* (Downers Grove, IL: Intervarsity Press, 1999), p. 44.

12 Paul Stanley. Telephone Interview. 17 August 2009.

Chapter 6

1 http://www.experienceproject.com/stories/Dont-Think-Anyone-Would-Care-If-I-Disappeared/2912047

2 http://www.childtrends.org/?indicators=adolescents-who-felt-sad-or-hopeless

3 http://www.newsmax.com/Newsfront/American-dream-economy-McClatchy-Marist/2014/02/14/id/552807/

4 Kenneth D. Kochanek, S.L. Murphy, Robert N. Anderson, and C. Scott, "Deaths: final data for 2002," *National Vital Statistics Reports, October 2004,* 12;53 (5):1-115.

5   http://www.cbsnews.com/8301-3445_162-2015684.html

6   http://www.businessinsider.com/advertisers-using-facial-recognition-technology-2013-5

7   Larry J. Nelson, Laura M. Padilla-Walker, and Jason S. Carroll, "I Believe it Is Wrong But I Still Do It": A Comparison of Religious Young Men Who Do Versus Do Not Use Pornography," *Psychology of Religion and Spirituality*, Vol. 2, No. 3, August 2010, pp. 137-147.

8   The other condition was drug use. Jeremy E. Uecker, Mark D. Regnerus, and Margaret L. Vaaler, "Losing My Religion: The Social Sources of Religious Decline in Early Adulthood," *Social Forces*, Vol. 85, No. 4, June 2007, pp. 1667-1692.

9   Playing off one of the best resources on sin and the Fall: Cornelius Plantinga, Jr., *Not the Way It's Supposed to Be: A Breviary of Sin* (Grand Rapids, MI: Eerdmans, 1995).

10 Mihaly Csikszentmihalyi, *Finding Flow* (New York: Basic, 1998), p. 69.

11 Peter J. Leithart, "No Heavenly Good," http://www.leithart.com/archives/003113.php

12 Peter Berger and Thomas Luckman, *The Social Construction of Reality: A Treatise in the Sociology of Knowledge* (New York: Doubleday, 1966), p. 163. Quoted in Steven Garber, *Fabric of Faithfulness* (Downers Grove, IL: InterVarsity, 2007), p. 173.

13 See Kathleen A. Kovner Kline, *Hardwired to Connect: The New Scientific Case for Authoritative Communities* (New York: Broadway Publications, 2003), p. 8. This crucial report was produced jointly by the YMCA of the USA, the Commission on Children at Risk, Dartmouth Medical School, and the Institute for American Values. The report's website says, "As an ideal type, an authoritative community has 10 main characteristics: 1) it is a social institution that includes children and youth; 2) it treats children as ends in themselves; 3) it is warm and nurturing; 4) it establishes clear boundaries and limits; 5) it is defined and guided at least partly by nonspecialists; 6) it is multigenerational; 7) it has a long-term focus; 8) it encourages spiritual and religious development; 9) it reflects and transmits a shared understanding of what it means to be a good person; 10) it is philosophically oriented to the equal dignity of all persons and to the principle of love of neighbor. Authoritative communities can be families with children, and all civic, educational, recreational, community service, business, culture and religious groups, that serve or include persons under the age of 18, that exhibit these characteristics." While it is possible for business and civic organizations to fulfill this function, by design they can almost never fulfill all 10 criteria. Churches, by definition, almost always do (obviously some churches do better than others).

14 Plato, *The Republic*, see especially Book 7 on the allegory of the cave. Full text at http://classics.mit.edu/Plato/republic.mb.txt

15 Titus Lucretius Carus, *On the Nature of Things, Book 2*. Full text at http://classics.mit.edu/Carus/nature_things.mb.txt

16 This is seen throughout the Old Testament. Khokmah is used in reference to the skilled craftsmen who built the temple in Exodus 35, those skilled in music (1 Kings 4:31-32) and performance (Jeremiah 9:17), military strategists and statesmen (Isaiah 10:13; 29:14; Jeremiah 49:7), magicians and soothsayers are considered wise men (Genesis 41:8; Isaiah 44:25), and those who could make difficult judicial decisions (2 Samuel 14:17, 20; 19:27).

17 Ursula M. Stuadinger and Monisha Pasupathi, "Correlates of Wisdom-related Performance in Adolescence and Adulthood: Age-graded Differences in 'Paths' Toward Desirable Development," *Journal of Research on Adolescence*, Vol. 13, No. 3, 2003, pp. 240.

18 Lars Tornstam, "Gerotranscendence: The Contemplative Dimension of Aging," *Journal of Aging Studies*, Vol. 11, No. 2, 1997, pp. 143-154.

19 Proverbs 10:1, 13:1, 13:20, and 1 Peter 5:5.

20 Brad Darrach, "Meet Shaky, the First Electronic Person," *Life*, November 20, 1970, 68.

21 See D.J.A. Clines, "The Image of God in Man," *Tyndale Bulletin*, Vol. 19, 1968, pp. 53-103 http://98.131.162.170//tynbul/library/TynBull_1968_19_03_Clines_ImageOf-GodInMan.pdf

22 In John 14:6, Jesus claimed to be the way (the basis for morality), the truth (the basis of what can be known), and the life (the aesthetic dimension that makes life worth living). In a very real way, he was the answer to the philosopher's quest.

23 Chap Clark, *When Kids Hurt: Help for Adults Navigating the Adolescent Maze* (Ada, MI: Baker Book House, 2009), p. 42.

Chapter 7

1 Thomas Friedman, "Israel Discovers Oil," *New York Times*, June 10, 2007.

2 Juergen Kneifel. Telephone Interview. 12 August 2009.

3 Irwin Altman and Dalmas Taylor, *Social Penetration: The Development of Interpersonal Relationships* (New York: Holt, Rinehart and Winston, 1973).

4 Joe Couch. Personal Interview. 14 June 2011.

5 Susan Hunt, "Spiritual Mothering: The Titus 2 Mandate for Women Mentoring Women," True Woman Conference. Chattanooga Convention Center, Chattanooga, TN. 26 March 2010.

6 Bill Roberson. Telephone Interview. 28 June 2011.

7 Lynn Harold Houg, quoted in Richard R. Wynn, Ex. Ed., *Lead On: A Mentor's Guide* (Englewood, CO: Emerging Young Leaders, Inc., 1998), p. 70.

Chapter 8

1 Diana West, *The Death of the Grown-Up: How America's Arrested Development Is Bringing Down Western Civilization* (New York: St. Martins Press, 2007), p. 1-2.

2 Chap Clark, *Hurt: Inside the World of Today's Teenagers* (Ada, MI: Baker Book House, 2005), p. 178.

3 Gunter Krallman, *Mentoring for Mission* (Franklin, TN: Authentic, 2003).

4 Christian Smith, *What Is a Person?* (Chicago: University of Chicago Press, 2010), p. 73.

5 Alan Loy McGinnis, *The Friendship Factor* (Minneapolis: Augsburg, 1979), p. 9.

6 John 15:15.

7 Miller McPherson, Lynn Smith-Lovin and Matthew Brashears, "Social Isolation in America: Changes in Core Discussion Networks Over Two Decades," *American Sociological Review*, V. 71, 2006, pp. 353–375.

8 Albert Mehrabian, "Communication Without Words," from *Psychology Today Magazine,* 1968, reprinted in C. David Mortensen, ed., *Communication Theory* 2nd ed., (New Brunswick, NJ: Transaction, 2008), p. 193.

9 See John 15-18 and Luke 22.

10 Jean E. Rhodes, *Stand By Me: The Risks and Rewards of Mentoring Today's Youth* (Cambridge, MA: Harvard University Press, 2002), p. 37.

11 Kenneth G. Van Meter, "The Order of Importance of Component Parts of the Biblical Worldview in Christian High School Students," George Fox University School of Education, Newberg, Oregon, 2009.

12 For more on Bill Perry's vital ministry for college students, visit http://www.recon-web.com

13 Interview with Parker Palmer, *Teaching By Heart: The Foxfire Interviews*, ed. Sara Day Hatton (New York: Teachers College Press, 2005), p. 74.

14 J.R. Kerr. Telephone Interview. 10 August 2009.

15 Stratford Sherman, "How tomorrow's leaders are learning their stuff," *Fortune*, November 27, 1995.

16 Mark 3:14-15, John 14:12, Matthew 10:16, Matthew 28:18-20. "Sending out" was a persistent characteristic of Jesus' ministry.

17 Here are just a few sources you'll want to check out to see what we mean about the paradigm shift in learning and growing: (1) Jim Collins and Jerry Porras demonstrated in *Built to Last* that stellar companies have one thing in common: a culture of succession management (Robert P. Gandossy and Nidhi Verma, "Passing the Torch of Leadership," *Leader to Leader Journal*, No. 40, Spring 2006); (2) Companies that don't prioritize leadership succession planning experience a steady attrition in talent and end up retaining people with outdated skills (Jeffrey M. Cohn, Rakesh Khurana and Laura Reeves, "Growing Talent as If Your Business Depended on It," *Harvard Business Review*, October 2005, p. 64); (3) Mentored executives are more likely to express great satisfaction with their career progress and are more likely to derive tremendous joy from their vocations (Adebowale Akande, "The Mentor Mystique: 'Everybody Who Makes It Has a Mentor or Mentors,'" *Equal Opportunities International*, 1993, p. 7); (4) Employees who are coached feel an increased ability to communicate confidently (Hilary B. Armstrong, Peter J. Melser and Julie-Anne Tooth, "Executive Coaching Effectiveness: A Pathway to Self-Efficacy," Institute of Executive Coaching, Sydney, Australia, 2007); (5) Companies that provided coaching realized improvement in productivity, quality, organizational strength, customer service and shareholder value. Customer complaints went down and executives who were coached were more likely to stay with the company (Business Wire, "Executive Coaching Yields Return on Investment of Almost Six Times Its Cost, Says Study," 4 July 2001); (6) A study of elite performers found that the key to their success was not innate ability, but supervised practice that started at a young age and continued for many years (K. Anders Ericsson and Neil Charness, "Expert Performance," *American Psychologist*, August 1994, p. 725); (7) Experiencing coaching was associated with enhanced mental health, quality of life and goal attainment (Anthony M. Grant, "The Impact of Life Coaching on Goal Attainment, Metacognition and Mental Health," *Social Behavior and Personality*, Vol. 31, No. 3, 2003, pp. 253-265).

18 See, for instance, Claudia M. Mueller and Carol S. Dweck, "Praise for Intelligence Can Undermine Children's Motivation and Performance," *Journal of Personality and Social Psychology*, Vol. 75, No. 1, 1998, pp. 33-52.

Chapter 9

1 Linda A. Hill, "Where will we find tomorrow's leaders?" *Harvard Business Review*, January 2008, p. 126.

2 Gunter Krallmann, *Mentoring for Mission*, (Waynesboro, GA: Authentic Media, 2003).

3 Elliot Aronson, "The Power of Self-Persuasion," *American Psychologist*, Vol. 54, Issue 11, November 1999, p. 882.

4 Ibid., throughout text.

5 This specific contrast came from a telephone interview with Tony Stoltzfus, 12 August 2009.

6 Ibid.

7 Olivero, G., Bane, K.D., & Kopelman, R.E., "Executive coaching as a transfer of training tool: Effects on productivity in a public agency," *Public Personnel Management*, 26(4), 1997, pp. 461-469.

8 Stoltzfus. Telephone Interview.

9 Annette Boorman. Telephone Interview. 23 June 2011.

10 Thao N. Le, "Age Differences in Spirituality, Mystical Experiences and Wisdom," *Aging & Society*, Vol. 28, 2008, pp. 383-411.

11 See "Still relevant after decades, the Beatles set to rock 9/9/09." http://www.cnn.com/2009/SHOWBIZ/Music/09/04/beatles.999/index.html?iref=newsearch

12 Chap Clark, *Hurt: Inside the World of Today's Teenagers* (Ada, MI: Baker Book House, 2005), p. 35.

Chapter 10

1 See Psalm 139.

2 See 1 Chronicles 12:32.

3 See Romans 8:20-21.

ABOUT THE AUTHOR

Dr. Jeff Myers

is president of Summit Ministries, a highly respected worldview training program whose tens of thousands of graduates are making a difference in politics, law, academics, medicine, science and business. In the last 20 years, Dr. Myers has become one of America's most respected authorities on youth leadership development. Focus on the Family founder, James Dobson, referred to him as "a very gifted and inspirational young leader." Evangelist Josh McDowell called him "a man who is 100 percent sold out to preparing the next generation to reflect the character of Christ in the culture." Through his appearances on Fox News and other media programs, Dr. Myers has become a fresh voice offering humor and insight from a Christian worldview. He holds a Doctor of Philosophy degree from the University of Denver and teaches leadership courses through CollegePlus and Belhaven University. Jeff and his family live in Colorado.

SUMMIT MINISTRIES

An alarming number of Christians stumble while in college, and around half will renounce their faith because they simply do not have a defense for what they believe. David Noebel founded Summit in 1962 to help ground Christians in their faith, enabling them to face the challenges that a post-Christian culture presents to followers of Jesus.

Summit equips Christians to think faithfully and engage courageously through conferences, curricula and content.

Conferences. Each of Summit's one-of-kind conference settings creates mentoring communities in which expert instructors equip students to fearlessly embrace and defend truth. Summit's renowned two-week programs for 16- to 21-year-old students take place every summer in Colorado and across the U.S.

Summit also offers Institutes — longer study programs with collegiate credits. Summit Semester serves as a gap-year program for students headed to top universities. Summit Oxford is a study-abroad program in which invited students study in one of three exclusive colleges of Oxford University. In each of these Institutes, students receive advanced worldview training and mentoring.

Curricula. With the goal of solid biblical thinking and cultural engagement, Summit has become a leading-edge provider of accessible, biblically faithful and academically credible curricula for Christian schools, homeschools and churches. Our seminal work *Understanding the Times* is one of the best-selling worldview textbooks of all time.

Content. Today, with its world-renowned faculty and under the direction of President Dr. Jeff Myers, Summit is viewed as one of the foremost leaders in training Christians to think faithfully and engage culture. Summit aims to provide a thorough grasp of the biblical, Christian worldview and prepare believers to analyze today's competing worldviews in the light of Truth. Summit provides a number of helpful resources including books, videos, a monthly Journal, original articles, streaming lectures and more.

Learn more at summit.org